PENGUIN BOOKS

MUGHAL INDIA

Dr G.H.R. Tillotson is a Fellow of Peterhouse, Cambridge, special-
izing in Indian architecture. His previous writing on this topic
includes *The Rajput Palaces* and *The Tradition of Indian Architecture*. He has been visiting India regularly since 1979 and has led
study tours to the sites covered in the present book.

ARCHITECTURAL series
GUIDES FOR TRAVELLERS

•

MUGHAL INDIA

G.H.R. TILLOTSON

720.954
TIL

PENGUIN BOOKS

PENGUIN BOOKS

Published by the Penguin Group
27 Wrights Lane, London W8 5TZ, England
Viking Penguin Inc., 40 West 23rd Street, New York 10010, USA
Penguin Books Australia Ltd, Ringwood, Victoria, Australia
Penguin Books Canada Ltd, 2801 John Street, Markham, Ontario, Canada L3R 1B4
Penguin Books (NZ) Ltd, 182-190 Wairau Road, Auckland 10, New Zealand

Penguin Books Ltd, Registered Offices: Harmondsworth, Middlesex, England

Designed and produced by Johnson Editions Ltd
15 Grafton Square, London SW4 0DQ

First published in Great Britain by Viking 1990
Published in Penguin Books 1991
10 9 8 7 6 5 4 3 2 1

Copyright © Johnson Editions Ltd, 1990
Text copyright © G. H. R. Tillotson, 1990
All rights reserved

Series conceived by Georgina Harding
Editor: Louisa McDonnell
Series design: Clare Finlaison
Design: Wendy Bann
Maps and plans: David Woodroffe
Picture research: Emma Milne
Index: Hilary Bird

Typesetting: DP Photosetting
Origination: Fotographics, London-Hong Kong
Printed in The Netherlands by Giethoorn, Meppel

CONTENTS

PREFACE

When the Mughals ruled India, their wealth and splendour were famous throughout the world, and their name is still a byword for absolute power. Conquering the north of the country early in the 16th century, they established the last and the greatest of India's Muslim imperial dynasties. In the ensuing centuries they oversaw the construction of numerous buildings of outstanding quality, including (most famously) the Taj Mahal.

This book is an introduction to this great architectural heritage, and is intended for the traveller. It aims in a short space to present some details of the buildings' history and design. This is a task not attempted since the guides written a century ago, by Stephen, Keene, Sanderson and Havell; the present book follows in their tradition, though often differing from them in matters of stylistic analysis.

Today, most foreign visitors to India, in search of Mughal buildings, begin in Delhi. They move on to Agra, from where they visit Fatehpur Sikri. As a result of this geographically logical progress, they tend to examine much of the development of Mughal architecture in reverse, visiting some of its best later examples first. For better companionship, this book follows the geographical not the historical sequence; some general comments about the development of the style are given in the Introduction, and a chronology is appended at the end.

(*Opposite*) A view of part of the palace at Fatehpur Sikri.

ITINERARY

All the major buildings discussed in the chapter on **Delhi** could be seen in two days, if the following programme is adopted:

Day 1
Morning — the Qutb Minar and Mehrauli; afternoon — Humayun's tomb and Nizamuddin;

Day 2
Morning — Shahjahanabad and the Red Fort; afternoon — Safdar Jang's tomb and the Purana Qila.

But because of the many lesser buildings which are mentioned in relation to these major sites, Delhi repays a more leisurely inspection. The visitor who is pressed for time might concentrate on the Qutb Minar, the Red Fort, the Jami Masjid (the principal mosque in Shahjahanabad), and Humayun's tomb.

Delhi contains, of course, much more of interest besides the Mughal architecture. There is a plentiful supply of earlier Islamic architecture. Apart from the Qutb Minar and Mosque (which are described here), the best examples include the 14th-century palace complex at Hauz Khas, and the assortment of 15th-century tombs concentrated in an area now laid out as the elegant and restful Lodi Gardens. A later contribution to the city's architecture are the buildings of New Delhi designed by Edwin Lutyens and Herbert Baker: these include what was formerly the Viceroy's House (now called Rashtrapati Bhawan) and the government Secretariats. The National Museum on Janpath contains a permanent display of a wide variety of Indian art, including some Mughal miniature paintings (it is closed on Mondays).

Most of the Mughal buildings in Delhi — like those in the other cities — are open to visitors every day during daylight hours. Some minor monuments have watchmen whose assistance may be required, and who should be tipped. Official entry fees are generally small. In some mosques which are still in use, tourists are not allowed to enter at times of prayer (which vary seasonally). Delhi's Red Fort is also open in the evenings for *Son et Lumière* performances (times

The interior of the Moti Masjid, Agra Fort.

vary seasonally and according to language).

Delhi is linked to **Agra** (200 km/125 miles to the south) by road, rail, and air (the flight takes 45 minutes, the fastest train 3 hours). All the Mughal buildings in Agra can be visited in 1½ days, allowing half a day each for the Fort, the Taj Mahal, and the other buildings described. A taxi is required for a visit to Sikandra. It is possible to see the Taj Mahal and the Fort on a day trip from Delhi, using the flight, the Taj Express train, or one of the many private coach services.

A full day should be reserved for even a cursory examination of **Fatehpur Sikri**. This lies 40 km (25 miles) west of Agra, and can be visited from there by car or State bus. For more earnest visitors, some accommodation is available locally.

Srinagar may be reached by air from Delhi. The railway goes only as far as Jammu (12 hours), from where buses go to Srinagar (another 12 hours). The two main Mughal gardens can be visited in half a day, though few when in Kashmir feel any need to hurry.

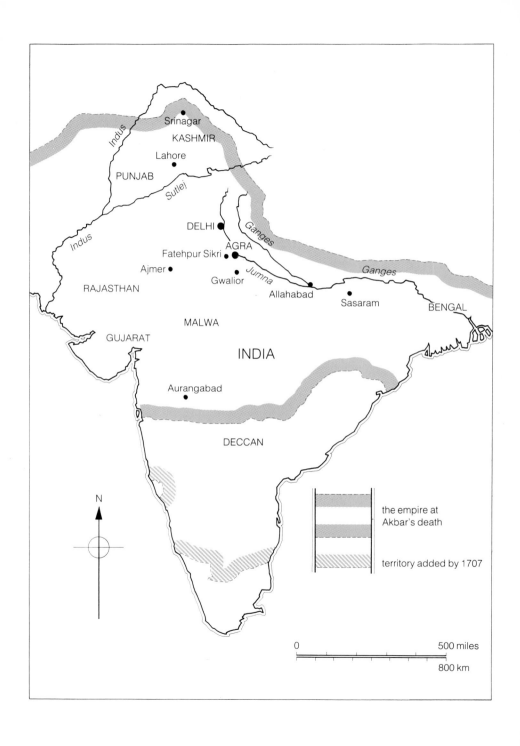

Srinagar

KASHMIR

Indus

Lahore

PUNJAB

Sutlej

Indus

DELHI

Ganges

AGRA

Fatehpur Sikri

Ajmer

Gwalior

Jumna

Ganges

RAJASTHAN

Allahabad

Sasaram

BENGAL

MALWA

GUJARAT

INDIA

Aurangabad

DECCAN

N

the empire at
Akbar's death

territory added by 1707

0   500 miles

800 km

INTRODUCTION
THE MUGHAL DYNASTY

In 1192, an Afghan sultan crossed the mountains of the Hindu Kush and the River Indus. His earlier visits to India had met with limited success, but on this occasion he defeated an alliance of Hindu forces which had assembled on the plain of Tarain under the command of the Chauhan Rajput monarch, Prithviraj III. The following year, the invading forces took possession of Prithviraj's former capital at Delhi.

Indian observers at the time might reasonably have seen nothing exceptional in this. Delhi had changed hands in the past: most recently, the outgoing Chauhans had taken it from another Rajput clan, the Tomars, only a few decades before. There had even been other hostile Muslims on the soil of the subcontinent. Nearly five centuries earlier, in 712, Arabs had conquered Sind — and so helped extend Islamic rule from southern Spain to western India within a century of the death of the Prophet. And early in the 11th century, another Afghan sultan, Mahmud of Ghazni, had made a series of raids into India, sacking such cities as Kanauj, Mathura and Somnath. But Mahmud had only ever stayed a year or so; he usually plundered until his army was satisfied, and then returned home (preferring the western climate), leaving the local population to sort themselves out and build up sufficient wealth to invite another raid. And like the Arabs before him, Mahmud had maintained lasting control only over western marginal regions. The new invader, Muhammad of Ghur, had similarly come and gone before, and even after his victory at Tarain he was soon recalled across the Hindu Kush by an emergency on his western frontier. But unlike his predecessors, he left behind a deputy — his former slave and general, **Qutb-ud-din Aibak** — who ensured a settled Islamic dominion over the newly acquired territory. Qutb-ud-din ruled Delhi faithfully, as a province and in his master's name, until Muhammad of Ghur's death in 1206; he then declared himself an independent ruler and so founded a new political entity, the Delhi sultanate. The secure establishment of Islamic power in a geographically central position was a novelty in India, and

(*Opposite*) The Mughal empire.

1

one which was to alter radically the course of the country's history and the development of her culture.

In the first place, it brought to an end the dominance of the Rajput clans. The **Rajputs** were a people of obscure (and probably diverse) origins, who formed part of the *kshatriya varna* or warrior group of the Hindu caste system. They had first risen to prominence in the period of turmoil following the death of the powerful emperor Harshavardhana in 647; since then they had dominated north Indian polity, dividing the area into a range of autonomous kingdoms. But the various clans who governed these kingdoms were always in competition with each other, in a struggle whose ceaselessness was ensured by the military ethic and the cult of valour which lay at the heart of Rajput civilization. With the loss of Delhi and other northern strongholds such as Kanauj, their activities were restricted to the westerly region now called Rajasthan.

In the three centuries following Muhammad's conquest, the Delhi sultanate was secured and enlarged. The dynasty established by Qutb-ud-din (known as the Slave dynasty because of the originally subservient position of its founder) did not, however, survive all this period. Islam did not have, any more than Hinduism, the power to impose political unity on its adherents, and even within the faith there was ample competition for a territorial prize such as the Delhi sultanate became. It passed from one Islamic hand to another, sometimes as a result of internal dissension, sometimes as a result of foreign invasion. Between 1206 and 1526 it was ruled by five Islamic dynasties, which were mostly Afghan or Turkish by origin. Successive sultans expanded the territory, especially eastwards to include Jaunpur and Bengal, and southwards to include Malwa, Gujarat and the Deccan; however, at any moment of weakness in the centre these gains could be lost again, as the local governors of the peripheral regions seized the opportunity to declare themselves independent rulers and to establish their own petty sultanates and dynasties. By the early 16th century, Islamic dominion in India was geographically almost as extensive as it would ever be, but it was not unified. None of the first five Islamic dynasties in Delhi was able to control all of the Islamic possessions at once. It took the power of the sixth and last dynasty to reunite the fragmented possessions and weld them into an empire. These great welders were the Mughals.

* * *

Unlike many of their predecessors on the Delhi throne, the Mughals were not Afghans; their homeland lay further north, in the area to the east of the Caspian Sea (an area now in southern Russia). The man who was to establish the Mughal dynasty in India, **Babur**, was a prince of distinguished lineage. He was descended on his mother's side from the 13th-century Mongol scourge known as Chengiz Khan (the name 'Mughal' refers to this connection since it is a Persian variant of 'Mongol'). On his father's side, Babur was descended from the scarcely less ferocious and infamous Timur (for long known to Western writers as Tamburlaine). Despite this ancestry, Babur's inheritance was nothing but a tiny kingdom — Farghana — and he not unnaturally felt that his destiny owed him more. He identified himself as a Timurid, and throughout much of his life his guiding ambition was the recapture of Timur's great capital, Samarkand. He did, in fact, three times succeed in taking Samarkand, but he could never hold it for long and eventually he conceded defeat and decided to look elsewhere for a kingdom. His designs on Samarkand had been inspired by what he took to be a legitimate (because ancestral) claim, and it was by the same reasoning that he now looked south, beyond the Hindu Kush to India, for Timur's many achievements had included a brief conquest of Delhi. In 1398 Timur's forces had swept into northern India and ravaged it. The exercise was more plundering raid than conquering invasion and Timur soon withdrew, but not before installing a new dynasty in power in Delhi — the Sayyids — who ruled for a while in Timur's name. Babur could therefore argue, if a little speciously, that by invading India he would merely be retaking what was his by right.

But more than a century had passed since Timur's raid, and in the meantime the Sayyids had been replaced by another dynasty, the Lodis. The current incumbent of the Delhi throne, Sultan Ibrahim Lodi, was not disposed to surrender his position simply out of respect for Babur's pedigree. Fortunately for Babur, he had, besides blood, a more persuasive advantage over the defender: gunpowder. It was with a relatively small force, but one armed with artillery, that Babur defeated Ibrahim Lodi at the battle of Panipat in April 1526. With that victory, Babur laid claim to the Delhi sultanate, but his position was still precarious:

A ruined palace in the fort of Chitor, the dominant Rajput stronghold (15th century).

having overcome the Islamic defence, he had next to subdue the still more considerable Hindu resistance. For he was immediately challenged by the assembled Rajput forces, under the command of Rana Sanga of Chitor who was reckoned by Babur one of the two greatest Hindu rulers. It was only after he had met and defeated this second and greater force — at the battle of Khanua in March 1527 — that he could consider the conquest achieved.

Only then, too, could the new landlord pause to examine the property he had acquired, and as he made his survey his reaction was more one of disappointment than of pride. Remembering his bewitching, ancestral Samarkand, he lamented in his diary that

> Hindustan is a country of few charms. Its people have no good looks; of social intercourse, paying and receiving visits, there is none; of genius and capacity none; of manners none; in handicraft and work there is no form or symmetry, method or quality; there are no good horses, no good dogs, no grapes, musk-melons or first-rate fruits, no ice or cold water, no good bread or cooked food in the bazaars, no hot baths, no colleges, no candles, torches or candlesticks.

Some modern visitors who, like Babur, are confident of the correctness of their own country's mores and are attached by custom to its comforts, arrive at similar estimations of India; and they cannot share the conqueror's consolation:

4

'Pleasant things of Hindustan are that it is a large country and has masses of gold and silver.'

Despite the brief, bitter outburst against India, Babur's writing more generally indicates a sensitive and enquiring mind. He was as much a poet and scholar as a soldier and statesman. His diary is one of the most valuable documents of Mughal India because, unlike the biographies of some of his successors, it was written not by a professional stylist or flattering courtier, but by the emperor himself for his own purposes. His aim was not to convey a sense of his own majesty but simply to record his perceptions, and this he did with taste, humour, enthusiasm, and sometimes also an artlessness which suggests an engaging modesty. One of his chief interests was natural history; after giving an account of his conquest of India, he devoted a long passage to the country's flora and fauna. His description of India's strangest animal is typical of his ingenuous style:

> The elephant is an immense animal and very sagacious. If people speak to it, it understands; if they command anything from it, it does it. Its value is according to its size; it is sold by measure; the larger it is, the higher its price. People rumour that it is heard of in some islands as 10 *qari* high [the *qari* is a unit which varies from 60–90 cm/2–3 ft] but in this tract it is not seen above 4 or 5. It eats and drinks entirely with its trunk; if it lose the trunk it cannot live. It has two great teeth in its upper jaw, one on each side of its trunk; by setting these against walls and trees, it brings them down; with these it fights and does whatever hard tasks fall to it. People call these ivory; they are highly valued by Hindustanis. The elephant has no hair. It is much relied on by Hindustanis, accompanying every troop of their armies. It has some useful qualities: it crosses great rivers with ease, carrying a mass of baggage, and three or four have gone dragging without trouble the cart of the mortar it takes four or five hundred men to haul. But its stomach is large; one elephant eats the corn of two strings of camels.

An avid gardener, Babur was also a connoisseur of fruits, and he describes those indigenous to his new kingdom with an expert's relish:

> Mangoes when good, are very good, but, many as are eaten, few are first-rate. They are usually plucked unripe and ripened in the house. Unripe, they make excellent condiments, and are also good preserved in syrup. Taking it altogether, the mango is the best fruit of Hindustan ... It is eaten in two ways: one is to

5

squeeze it to a pulp, make a hole in it, and suck out the juice — the other, to peel it and eat it like a peach.

The detail in passages like these has led some readers to wonder for whose benefit Babur thought he was writing, since clearly the information he supplies is superfluous to anyone who lives in or is familiar with India. The very question misjudges Babur: he did not write for any audience,

Babur laying out a garden; from an illustrated copy of his memoirs, the *Babur-nama*.

but for himself. He is on a level with the modern traveller who is moved to record his experiences in a diary without supposing that his observations are so original as to be of interest to others. Paradoxically, it is just this parity which now makes Babur's writing accessible and delightful to a wide audience.

The diary aside, there survives less material evidence of Babur's achievements than of those of his successors. Little remains, in particular, of his building projects, so that he will not feature largely in the following pages.

He did not have to suffer the deprivations of life in India for long, as he died in 1530, four years after his invasion. He was succeeded by his son **Humayun**, an engaging but irresolute character who temporarily lost control of the empire and so nearly ended the Mughal dynasty almost as soon as it had begun. Aesthetic, nervous and clever, Humayun could on occasions exert himself with some success, but as often destroyed his own achievements through indecision or loss of interest. In 1540, he was dislodged from the Delhi throne by the Muslim ruler of Bihar and Bengal, Sher Khan. The usurper ruled from Delhi as Sher Shah Sur and was succeeded by his son Islam Shah; but this interregnum was brought to an end in 1555 when Humayun, who had in the meantime been a mendicant exile in Persia, regained control. He died in an accident in January of the following year, leaving the empire in the hands of his thirteen-year-old son, Akbar.

Akbar (r. 1556–1605), the greatest of the Great Mughals, whose very name means 'great', was in a sense the true founder of the Mughal empire. The substantial achievements of his grandfather, Babur, faded to a prelude beside his own. For it was Akbar who united the whole of northern India under Mughal rule (down to a line from Bombay to Puri) and who developed fully the empire's bureaucracy, and its systems of government, taxation and communication. He brought independent sultanates such as Malwa and Gujarat back under central control, and subdued most of the Rajput states.

The figure and personality of Akbar loom over the Mughal period to the extent that there is a temptation to identify the empire itself with him. Nor would that be altogether the lazy shorthand of retrospect, since it is evident that many of his contemporaries saw him as the embodiment of the empire,

not just its leader. This view was encouraged, first, by his physical strength and courage. When, early in his reign, his foster-brother murdered a minister within the palace precincts, the unarmed Akbar disabled the retreating assassin with a single knock-out punch. Such episodes entered a catalogue of the emperor's superhuman exploits, and so helped construct the myth which located the source of all imperial power in his person.

Similarly, though many of the leisure activities of late medieval India entailed some measure of danger and violence, Akbar liked to enhance the standard dose. Ranking high among the pleasures of the Mughals was the sport of setting animals such as elephants, tigers and buffalo, to fight against each other. Sometimes the competing animals were of the same species, to ensure an even contest; and sometimes (in a spirit of enquiry typical of the early Mughals) animals of different species were set to fight, in order that their relative strengths and skills in combat might be compared. Such contests were normally viewed from a safely elevated position, but Akbar's personal variation on the sport was to seat himself on the back of one of the animals, to get a better view. Akbar's friend and biographer, Abul Fazl, recorded how hazardous this practice could be:

> One day he mounted the elephant called Lakhna, which was an exhibitor of terrific rage, at a time when it was at the height of its ferocity, evil nature and man-killing, and made it engage with an elephant like itself, so that the proudest were surprised. The elephant Lakhna ... was victorious and was madly pursuing the other when suddenly its foot ... fell into a deep ditch, and in its furious condition ... it made great struggles and movements. ... Then, when cries awoke on every side, and the hearts of the loyal melted within them, the holy personality was moved from its place, and his sky-brushing foot became fixed in the rope of the elephant's neck.... His Majesty, with a heart which can throw the noose of courage on the heavens, and a palm which had God's help in its fingers, firmly seized the rope, and having hold of the strong cable of this Divine protection remained strong of heart and serene in soul.

As Abul Fazl explained, such behaviour arose not only from Akbar's spirit of adventure but also from a serious political motive: he hoped by these displays of valour to intimidate his courtiers and so banish all thought of disloyalty.

At an early age, Akbar's relish of active life precluded

(*Opposite*) Akbar directing the siege of Ranthambor; from a manuscript of the *Akbarnama*.

(*Opposite*) Tiger hunting near Gwalior; from a manuscript of the *Akbarnama*.

study, and unlike his literary forbears, he never fully learned to read or write. But even when he later took to bookish pursuits, his illiteracy was not in practice a severe handicap, for he could find others to read to him and he was equipped with a powerful intellect. He had a particular interest in religious and mystical issues, a study which he pursued deeply during the 1570s when his court was established at the newly-built capital at Fatehpur Sikri. He listened to Muslim divines disputing on religious matters, and subsequently broadened their debates by introducing representatives of other religions. His interest in other men's beliefs raised the hopes of some Jesuits from Goa (who mistook interest for sympathy) and alarmed the *ulama* or orthodox scholars at the court, who considered him a heretic. Indeed he was, in so far as he abandoned respect for religious authority unchallenged by the individual intellect. His views were empirical, not dogmatic. When he expressed the opinion, based on personal experience, that one should bathe before making love, the orthodox scholar Badauni was shocked, for Islamic tradition advised that the bath should come after.

The chief product of Akbar's religious study was a new religion of his own invention, the Din Ilahi, which drew together ideas from disparate sources. Though Akbar hoped that it would become the single religion of the empire, in fact it was probably never espoused by more than a few of his close associates; it was an eccentric project and it did not survive him. It was partly based, however, on a sound political doctrine: Akbar was seeking to erase the most conspicuous distinction between the rulers of the empire and the mass of its population; he hoped to unite its various peoples in a common faith. Here, then, was another reason to see Akbar as an embodiment of the empire itself, as the eclecticism of his personal vision reflected and was informed by the diversity of the land that he ruled.

Although the Din Ilahi failed to become popular, the sympathy for the empire's citizens that underlay it, also informed more important policies, so that Akbar's rule could fairly be called enlightened. Most notably, in spite of his hopes for the Din Ilahi, he respected the religions of those whom he conquered. The early Islamic invasions of India had not led to forcible, large-scale conversions of the population to Islam, but they had involved a measure of

iconoclasm; Akbar actively sought to guarantee freedom of worship and to protect temples from destruction.

And the religious tolerance was matched in the political sphere. When the Rajput states were subdued, for example, their rulers were not deposed: the states were regarded collectively as a province of the empire (with a provincial capital at Ajmer), but the borders of the individual states were maintained; and as long as they paid their taxes to the imperial treasury, the Rajput rajas were left in command of their ancestral homelands. The reason for this policy was that Akbar looked to the Rajput rajas to supply troops and to serve as commanders in the imperial forces, or as governors of the empire's remoter provinces such as Bengal. He knew that the stability of the empire would be more secure if the experience and the celebrated courage of the Rajputs were harnessed in support of it, rather than pitted against it. Granted religious freedom and a degree of political auto- nomy, many Rajput rajas were pleased to take advantage of the career opportunities offered to them. They saw the empire not as a foreign domination but as an enterprise in which many could co-operate, and from which many could benefit. True, they had to spend much time away from their capitals, but they were rewarded for their services with grandiose titles and privileges. They joined the upper ranks of the *mansabdar* system. Something between an aristo- cracy and a bureaucracy, this body administered the empire. Its structure was essentially military: each office — even a civil one — had attached to it a rank, which specified the number of men whom the holder was required to be able to put into the field. To ensure a high quality of officer, appointment was not hereditary but lay in the emperor's gift; and the *mansabdars* were paid in cash not in land, so that their personal influence was limited.

Another means by which Akbar won the allegiance of local rulers was marrying Indian princesses. As Abul Fazl explained: 'His Majesty forms matrimonial alliances with the princes of Hindustan, and of other countries; and secures by these ties of harmony, the peace of the world'. The situation was in fact not always quite as harmonious as this account implies. Despite the mutual benefits to be derived from co- operation, the volatile Rajput character ensured that rela- tions with the centre tended to be uneasy. But when any Rajput raja rebelled — as many were frequently disposed to do — others were set against him. The Rajputs, rarely averse to fighting each other, could be encouraged in this, if loyal supporters were promised parts of the rebels' territory. By such tactics, the Mughals maintained control of the Rajput states. Control was essential, not only for the stability of the empire as a whole but also to keep open trade routes, for the Rajput states lay between the Mughal capitals and the ports of Gujarat — the Mughals' points of contact with the rest of the Islamic world.

Of the Rajput clans, only the Sisodias consistently resisted the tempting rewards of succumbing to Mughal suzerainty. Though Akbar sacked their fortress capital of Chitor in 1567, they were undaunted: they simply founded a new capital, at Udaipur. They resisted Mughal dominance until the reign of his successor, and even then they disdained active service for the Mughals, considering that it would involve an intolerable loss of dignity. For the most part, they were allowed to get away with a minimal show of their subservient position. The Kachwahas of Amber, on the other hand, were most ready to align themselves with the imperial overlord; Raja Man Singh of Amber, especially, became a notable imperial commander. His aunt married Akbar and bore the emperor's son, Jahangir. The future emperor and Man Singh were therefore cousins — and they became also brothers-in-law when Jahangir reinforced the alliance by marrying Man Singh's sister.

The reign of **Jahangir** and that of his son **Shah Jahan** together covered the first half of the 17th century, and marked the long summer of Mughal rule. The relative political stability of the period was as much the legacy of Akbar as the fruit of their own exertions; they lacked his energy and vision, but it was enough that they were competent in tending what he had established. The period saw little further expansion of the empire's domains; a continuous campaign against the independent Muslim sultanates of the Deccan, on the empire's southern border, achieved little in terms of territory. Failure in such campaigns did not greatly matter: they were generally undertaken not in response to particular threats, nor to satisfy real needs, but through the unquestioned assumption that expansion was desirable. The Mughal forces were successful in the more critical work of supressing the usual periodic revolts by native rajas within the empire.

14

Command of the imperial forces was in this period often put in the hands of the heir, while the emperor remained at the capital. In Jahangir's reign, the young Shah Jahan enjoyed an impressive military career, achieving the long-sought suppression of the Sisodia Rajputs in 1614. Later, during his own reign, he appointed his son Aurangzeb as viceroy of the empire's southern districts. But this period of greater responsibility for the young was also one of rebellion within the imperial family. Jahangir had spent the last years of his father's reign in continual half-hearted rebellion; soon after he attained the throne, he had to teach a little humility to his elder son, Khusrau, and later faced a more prolonged rebellion by Shah Jahan. When Shah Jahan eventually inherited the throne (in a legal manner), he reduced the chances of further contest by dispatching his surviving brother (he had killed Khusrau already, and another had died of drink); but this fratricide and rebellion rebounded on him in time, when his own son cited them in justification of the next family quarrel.

Such behaviour was not greatly exceptional among Indian ruling houses of the time, and if taken as offering a clue to the personalities involved would be misleading; for in spite of the atrocities which he committed against his kin, Shah Jahan is a considerably more sympathetic figure than his father. Contemporary accounts portray Jahangir as a curious compound of cruelty and sensitivity, unpredictable in mood. He wrote his memoirs himself — like his ancestor, Babur — and revealed a similar capacity for delighted observation, especially of natural history. He was dominated by his favourite wife, Nur Jahan, whom he habitually consulted in matters of administration, to the vexation of many who had to negotiate with him, but probably also to the advantage of the empire. Shah Jahan was similarly devoted to one wife above all, Mumtaz Mahal, but she died shortly after his accession. Lacking both the cruelty and the subtlety of his father, Shah Jahan was a mellower character, a connoisseur and a sybarite.

The period in which these two men ruled was one of surpassing cultural achievement. Both inherited from Babur a love of gardens, and they embellished Lahore and the valley of Kashmir with formal gardens in the Persian paradise tradition which their ancestor had introduced into India. But Jahangir was a patron most especially of miniature painting.

(*Opposite*) Jahangir with the head of his rival, Malik Ambar.

The Mughal painting atelier had already been productive for some time. It had been established by Humayun, who had brought masters from the Persian court, on his return from exile. In Akbar's reign, the size and output of the atelier was enormously increased. Indian artists were attracted to the court, where they trained in the Persian idiom and contributed aspects of their own traditions. Much of the subject-matter at this time was political or historical: Akbar commissioned illustrations to histories of Mughal rule, such as the official account of his own reign, the *Akbarnama*, and illustrations of other Muslim histories and books of legend. A reflection of the emperor's broader religious interests is seen in the depictions of scenes from Hindu epics, such as the *Mahabharata*, which illustrate the translations of those works that he had ordered. Of course all these themes necessarily involve the frequent depiction of men and women. The Islamic tradition which forbids the representation of living forms (especially human and animal) arose from the perception that such work arrogates to men the creative role of God; but in India (as in other parts of the Islamic world) the respect which the ban received was somewhat selective. Mughal architectural ornament concentrates on arabesques and geometrical and floral designs; but this is a sign of the force not of religious but of artistic tradition. That the Mughals had no objection to breaking the ban is evident from the paintings, where it is happily ignored. Akbar, it appears, felt some need to justify his position on the matter; according to Abul Fazl, he told his courtiers:

> There are many that hate painting; but such men I dislike. It appears to me as if a painter had quite peculiar means of recognizing God; for a painter in sketching anything that has life, and in devising its limbs, one after the other, must come to feel that he cannot bestow individuality upon his work, and is thus forced to think of God, the giver of life.

Under Jahangir's direction, Mughal painting acquired a greater subtlety of both content and style. The court at this period had some contact with the West, and the European merchants and diplomats who attended the emperor in the hope of securing trading agreements, introduced the Mughal painters to Western art; the influence of its realism qualified the legacy of the Persian tradition. In the pursuit of higher quality, Jahangir reduced the number of artists in his

A nilgai; attributed to Jahangir's celebrated natural history painter, Mansur.

employment, and he encouraged a cult of technical skill. Formerly, particular paintings were usually produced by co-operative groups of artists, but now they were the work of individual masters. These masters concentrated not on sets of literary illustrations, but on single works. The dominant subjects were natural history (reflecting the emperor's personal interest) and portraiture. Depictions of the emperor himself include a number of recondite, allegorical works which illustrate Jahangir's fantasies of power.

Mughal painting continued to flourish under Shah Jahan, though the chief enthusiasms of this ruler were for jewellery and architecture. He collected gems with an unparalleled cupidity, and in the commissioning of the celebrated peacock throne his connoisseurship verged on vulgarity. His taste in architecture, though, was flawless. In the memorial to his beloved wife, Mughal architecture reached a zenith of sober splendour, and gave the world one of its most famous buildings.

Late in 1657, Shah Jahan fell ill and so provoked a civil war, as his four sons competed for the throne. By the following summer, the third son, **Aurangzeb**, had emerged victorious. The contest was a little premature, as Shah Jahan recovered from his illness; he lived for a further eight years under a house arrest imposed by his son. Among the brothers, Aurangzeb was in many respects the most able, but he was not perhaps the most fit to govern, and his long reign (1658–1707) saw the beginning of the process of the empire's disintegration. That process had two immediate causes. One was the continuing campaign in the Deccan: this became an all-consuming preoccupation in Aurangzeb's reign, and though he met with greater success than his predecessors, the empire was thereby extended beyond limits readily manageable without a modern system of communication. The other cause was Aurangzeb's reversal of his ancestor's policy towards the Rajputs and other Hindu subjects. Akbar, the empire-builder, had allowed temple construction to proceed unhindered and had abolished the *jizya*, the Islamic tax on heathen worship; Aurangzeb encouraged the destruction of temples and reimposed the *jizya*. But religious tolerance was fundamental to the success of the empire that Akbar founded: it was much more than the return for Rajput allegiance; it made all the emperor's subjects equal citizens and so turned an Islamic occupation into an acceptable, respected government. The abandonment of tolerance alienated the Rajputs, who no longer respected the empire; they were still not united in rebellion against it, but they were now even less dependable, less willing as its helpmates.

This change is registered in a letter to Aurangzeb from one of his sons, the young Prince Akbar (so named after his great-great-grandfather). Prince Akbar had rebelled against his father and formed an alliance with a Rajput force; in his letter, he cited his great ancestor in justifying his trust of the Rajputs, recalling how 'Emperor Akbar, peace be on him, strengthening the ties of alliance with them, conquered the whole of India and on their strength made his empire firm'.

But in Aurangzeb's reign, the young prince complained, 'the inhabitants of the place find themselves unable to praise and bless their king'. The young Akbar, like his illustrious namesake, did not base his estimation of a man's ability on his religion. This endeared him to the Rajputs, but his rebellion was not successful and he died in exile.

Aurangzeb's policies were inspired by a personal religious piety which earned him the respect of some contemporary Muslim observers (and of some later historians). Quite apart from the calamitous effects it had on the empire, his zeal led him to adopt a somewhat puritanical attitude to art, so that in his reign imperial patronage of the arts (and especially of painting and music) was substantially reduced, and many artists left the court to seek employment elsewhere. Mughal architecture had already reached its peak under Shah Jahan, and from now on its decline kept pace with that of the empire itself.

Aurangzeb in old age.

When Aurangzeb eventually died in 1707, he was succeeded by his second son, **Bahadur Shah**, who was already an old man and who survived only another five years. There then followed in rapid succession a series of weak men who could do nothing to reverse the failing fortunes of Mughal power. Their weakness incited the avidity of foreigners. First, in 1739, Nadir Shah of Persia invaded India and sacked Delhi. He did not stay; he had come not to rule but to take home the accumulated wealth of Mughal power, and to leave the empire in a disarray from which it could not recover. And with the decline of the authority of the centre, the regions once again assumed power to themselves: first, the hard-won provinces of the Deccan broke away, and they were soon followed by others such as Lucknow in the north, and Gujarat and Sind in the west.

The widespread loss of confidence in the imperial enterprise which had been inspired by Aurangzeb's policies, now ensured that few had any interest in preserving it. On the contrary, those policies had spawned new forces for its destruction. In the Punjab, the formerly pacifist Sikhs had been converted into a militaristic brotherhood; while in northern and central India, the Jats and the Marathas — low-caste Hindu agriculturalists — had similarly been transformed into martial peoples. Much of the 18th century was a seemingly chaotic (and certainly complex) period in which all of these forces and the Rajputs jostled for place. They competed with each other as much as with the Mughal forces, though sometimes temporary alignments were formed to attain short-term goals. The Marathas became a potent but dangerous tool in the settling of Rajput internecine disputes, as those rajas who sought Maratha assistance against their neighbours often found themselves unable to control their energetic allies, and the Marathas had no scruples about taking advantage of the weak.

The shifting military allegiances ensured that no power base was secure, no force achieved lastingly any more than regional control. The Marathas came closest to overall dominance, but their hopes of it were extinguished in 1761 by another temporarily visiting plunderer, the Afghan Ahmad Shah Abdali. By the end of the century, power over large areas was concentrated in the hands of a new force which was neither indigenous nor neighbouring: a force which, not long before, few Indian rulers could have considered a serious rival, since it was no more than a group of foreign traders. The East India Company had opened a new chapter in the subcontinent's history.

Troops under the command of General Lake captured the Mughal capital cities of Delhi and Agra in 1803. Even this action did not altogether remove the Mughals from India's political map. The dynastic line continued for another half century. The last of the Mughal emperors, styled 'Kings of Delhi' by the British, were in effect even less than that title implied, for they controlled no more than Delhi's fort. Their occupation of it was tolerated by the British who were, as ever, sentimental about royal tradition and attracted by Eastern glamour. But even British humour was exhausted in 1857 when the octogenarian Bahadur Shah II was made the figurehead of the sepoy mutiny. After the suppression of the mutiny, Bahadur Shah was exiled to Rangoon, and his imperial title and vestigial power were abruptly ended.

Mughal architecture

Mighty fortresses have been raised, which protect the timid, frighten the rebellious, and please the obedient. Delightful villas, and imposing towers have also been built. They afford excellent protection against cold and rain, provide for the comfort of the princesses of the Harem, and are conducive to that dignity which is so necessary for worldly power.

The early-Mughal 'Barber's Tomb' in Delhi.

Thus the court chronicler, Abul Fazl, described Akbar's building policy, characteristically noticing especially the political expedient involved. As his account implies, the Mughal forts and palaces were much more than imperial residences: they served as emblems of power and wealth, designed to dazzle and cow the native rajas who attended their overlord's court. This political function, as well as changes in taste, ensured that the building programme was lavish and continuous; Akbar's successors were not content with the palaces that he bequeathed to them, but built their own as well, with little regard to cost. Sometimes they even demolished earlier structures to make space for new ones; for although the Mughal emperors were proud of their dynastic heritage, each sought to mould the court in his own manner, and give his own reign a unique character.

Apart from forts and palaces, the two other most important types of Mughal building are mosques and tombs. Both, in function, are associated with the Muslim religion, though not with its scriptures. The Koran makes no prescriptions about the form or arrangement of the mosque, and indeed any such building is inessential. A Muslim may pray anywhere; the only specification is that he must face towards Mecca while doing so. The Koran discusses the *qibla*, or direction of prayer, which is usually indicated in a mosque by the rear wall of the sanctuary. But the form and other details of the mosque have grown up by tradition; the relation of the sanctuary to the courtyard, for example, is allegedly based on a typical Arab house, such as that in Medina used by the Prophet himself.

The tomb as an architectural type has even less connection with scripture than the mosque has. Grandiose structures such as the Mughals built are in fact expressly forbidden, since according to Muslim law a grave should be covered only by earth and bricks. Like the insistence that art should be aniconic, this law has been widely flouted. Grand Islamic tombs commonly have entrances without doors, so that the interior is open to the outside air, and it has been suggested that this arrangement was devised to satisfy the letter of the law while evading its real import. Such tortuous attempts to reconcile artistic aspiration with religious tradition, serve as a reminder that Islam is not a cultural monolith: the sultans and emperors who have ruled the Muslim world have generally been blessed with a far greater aesthetic sensitivity than were the Prophet and his immediate followers, on whose ideas their religious tradition was founded. That Islam should engender distinctive architectural qualities and styles, which would then become famous throughout the world, is not a circumstance which would have greatly delighted the Prophet, who once described architecture as 'the most unprofitable thing that eats up the wealth of a believer'.

Those responsible for the design and construction of the Mughal buildings were for the most part anonymous. This reflects the low social status accorded to them; credit for architectural achievements was given to the patron. But it also reflects the fact that designs were generally the product not of individuals but of groups working co-operatively. Contemporary accounts usually record the names only of the local officials appointed to manage the work-force. The design process involved a hierarchy of craftsmen, with various grades of skill, but there was no essential distinction between the functions of designer and builder: unlike in contemporary Europe, the men who worked the stone were executing their own, not other men's ideas. Their preparatory plans have not survived; and although it is clear that for the major parts some were made, for much of the work plans would not have been required, since the craftsmen worked out the details of their design on site.

Another problem regarding Mughal architecture's relation to a wider Islamic context concerns its style. Though the Mughals were foreign invaders of India, their architecture is not a wholly alien art-form imported complete; they did not simply construct Central Asian buildings on Indian soil. Their successors as imperial masters, the British, did import an alien style, peppering India with examples of Western classical design. But the British empire in India was an outpost, and the men and ideas that shaped it were continually supplied by a parent country. The Mughal empire was of a quite different kind, for Babur's invasion had been prompted in part by the loss of his Central Asian homeland, which never returned to Mughal control. So the Mughals were entirely transplanted; they were severed from their cultural roots, whose influence swiftly diminished, and they had to draw on more local resources. Furthermore, the first two Mughal emperors, Babur and Humayun, in fact built very little, having little opportunity; it was not until the reign of Akbar that the Mughal building programme became highly productive, so that time as well as politics divided Mughal architecture from any Timurid heritage.

This is not to deny that the essential character of Mughal architecture is Islamic and foreign. The emperors imported many ideas, and sometimes even architects, from neighbouring parts of the Muslim world, such as Persia. But they depended very considerably on India's indigenous craftsmen and builders. For India had an architectural tradition of its own, which had been developing over many centuries, in the temples and palaces of Buddhists and Hindus. With its deep and figurative stone-carving, its often elementary engineering, and a preference for organic rather than mathematical form, this indigenous tradition differed fundamentally in character from the rarefied geometry typical of most Islamic design. But this difference did not prevent Muslim patrons from employing Indian masons in the construction of their mosques and tombs. The native builders were able to adjust in some measure to the new requirements and design ideals, but they never forgot their inherited traditions, and they put aspects of these to the service of the new overlords. The result was the propagation of a new kind of architecture, an Islamic tradition distinct from any elsewhere. The popular view that Mughal architecture is Persian in style, is therefore not true: it has certain features, such as the pointed arch, which are characteristic of Islamic design

The Jagadambi
temple at Khajuraho
(Hindu, c. 1000 AD).

(whose fountain-head is Persia); but it developed as a
distinct Islamic tradition. Aware of — and partly influenced
by — Persian design, it remained different, because of the
local influences.

Earlier Muslim rulers in India had, of course, faced the
same situation, so that in fact India already had its own
Islamic tradition which had been developing there for three
centuries, before the advent of the Mughals. Mughal
architecture was therefore not a novel import, abruptly
introduced, but the continuation of an established Indo-
Islamic tradition, which had been initiated by Muhammad
Ghuri's deputy, Qutb-ud-din Aibak, at the end of the 12th
century, and which had always depended on the contribution of Indian craftsmen.

The degree of Hindu contribution at any particular
moment was variable. Akbar, consistently with his other
views, was an especial enthusiast of Hindu craftsmanship
and design. Although some of the buildings of his reign are
markedly Islamic (severe and simple in outline, making
dramatic use of the pointed arch) many are almost entirely
Hindu in style, especially his palace buildings in Agra and
Fatehpur Sikri. In the reign of Shah Jahan (the other most
prolific patron among the Mughals) the two traditions were

resolved to form a new one, and the distinctive, mature Mughal style was achieved. It is commonly argued that, with its frequent use of Hindu forms, Akbar's architecture displays a cultural synthesis, while Shah Jahan's returns to a more purely Persian style. This view will be argued against in this book: the mixture of Islamic and Hindu forms in Akbar's buildings can be exciting and creative, but not every mixture is a synthesis; in Mughal architecture it is not Akbar's but Shah Jahan's buildings which achieve a proper fusion of the disparate sources. Their appearance of purity derives from this success, for the purity is not Persian but Mughal.

In addition to this development, Shah Jahan's buildings are also distinguished by a much greater refinement, especially in the decoration. The robust stone patchwork of Akbar's period gave way to exquisite and delicate inlay of semi-precious stones. The richness, though, is always held in balance. The materials might be lavish and colourful, but the forms are chaste and simple. This combination is character-istic of mature Mughal design: it is a feature of the period's applied arts and *objets d'art* as much as of its buildings. In a later period, the ornament becomes florid; architectural forms are elongated to enhance their elegance, but they lose their strength. The exaggeration of flourishes first disguises and then destroys the clarity of outline, and the style is launched on a protracted but irreversible decline.

Shah Jahan's wine cup, in white nephrite jade.

DELHI
THE AXIS OF EMPIRE

Delhi's importance as a major city in India is of long standing. Legend and some slight evidence identify one portion of it as Indraprastha, the capital of the heroes of the great epic of Hinduism, the *Mahabharata*, and so retrace the city's history into the vaguely charted regions of proto-history. Much later it was the capital of the Tomar Rajputs, and was subsequently held by the Chauhan Rajput ruler, Prithviraj III. But little architectural vestige of this early Hindu rule now remains, as following Muhammad of Ghur's defeat over

Delhi
1. Chandni Chowk;
2. Red Fort;
3. Shahjahanabad;
4. Jami Masjid;
5. Faiz Bazar;
6. Connaught Place;
7. Rashtrapati Bhawan (formerly Viceroy's House);
8. National Museum;
9. India Gate;
10. Purana Qila;
11. Safdar Jang's tomb; 12. Lodi gardens;
13. Nizamuddin;
14. Humayun's tomb;
15. road to Qutb Minar and Mehrauli;
16. road to Mathura.

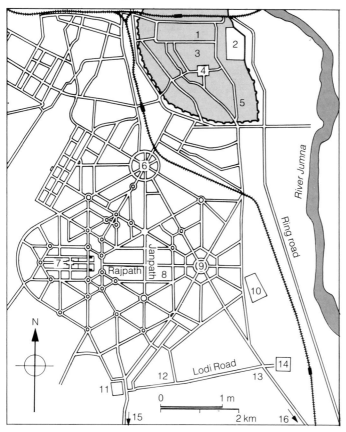

(*Opposite*)
The Qutb Minar.

27

Prithviraj III in 1192, the city became the centre of Islamic dominion in north India.

The successive Islamic dynasties which ruled from Delhi between the 12th and 19th centuries, built there a succession of capitals, the so-called seven cities of Delhi, which stand not one on top of another, but side by side, spread out over a large plain on the west bank of the River Jumna. The first of the seven cities was established by Muhammad of Ghur's deputy, Qutb-ud-din Aibak, on the site of Prithviraj's capital; indeed, it is still usually known as the Fort of Rai Pithora (after Prithviraj's alias). The cities built by some of Qutb-ud-din's successors lie in the vicinity in varying stages of ruin: next came Siri to the north, Tughluqabad to the east, and Jahanpannah immediately to the north; and then later and further north, Firoz Shah Kotla, the Purana Qila, and finally Shahjahanabad — the last, built by and named after the mid-17th-century Mughal emperor.

Following a hiatus after the collapse of Mughal power, Delhi was again restored to a pre-eminent position when the capital of the British Empire in India was transferred there from Calcutta in 1912. With the transfer of power in 1947, it became the capital of the Indian Republic.

An examination of the Mughal architecture of the city might suitably be prefaced by a consideration of the Qutb Minar and Mosque — the earliest major Islamic buildings on Indian soil, and among the most spectacular.

THE QUTB MINAR AND MOSQUE

A road leading southwards out of New Delhi passes a number of ruined forts. The first, to the east or left of the road after 6½ km (4 miles), is that of Siri, Delhi's second Islamic city. Soon after, the road penetrates the walls of Jahanpannah, the fourth Delhi. Finally, after 11 km (7 miles), it reaches a complex of ancient Hindu fortifications: an outer ring, the Fort of Rai Pithora, built by the Chauhan Rajputs in the 12th century, and an inner citadel, the Lal Kot, built a century earlier by the Tomar Rajputs. It was this Rajput fort which Muhammad of Ghur's forces conquered in 1193, and here that they established the first Islamic city of Delhi, with Qutb-ud-din as its first resident sultan. Within the innermost recess of the old Rajput citadel, Qutb-ud-din built a mosque and a tower; and these, together with certain associated buildings, are all that survive of his city.

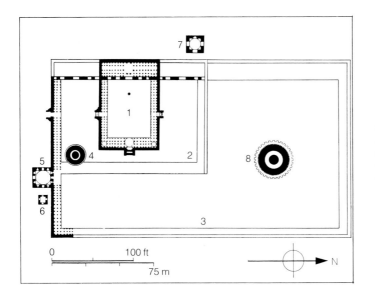

The Qutb mosque complex
1. original mosque of Qutb-ud-din;
2,3. extensions by Iltutmish and Ala-ud-din (not completed and largely ruined);
4. Qutb Minar;
5. Alai Darwaza;
6. Imam Zamin's tomb; 7. Iltutmish's tomb; 8. Alai Minar.

As it is seen now, the mosque is surrounded by later additions; the oldest part lies at the central core. This is a large paved court, bounded on the west side by a high screen of five pointed arches and on the other sides by a cloister (somewhat ruined on the south side). This was originally the whole of the mosque, built by Qutb-ud-din between 1193 and 1198. The early Islamic invaders were zealous iconoclasts; they raised this first mosque on the former site of twenty-seven Hindu and Jain temples which they demolished, and the mosque was given the appropriately intimidating epithet, Quwwatu'l Islam: the Might of Islam. The temples have not disappeared altogether without trace, since fragments of them were used in the construction of the mosque. In particular, the cloister is composed of undisguised temple columns. Their rich decoration includes emblems of Hindu worship, such as the bell and chain, and even some figure sculpture. That this traditional Hindu decoration was left intact when the columns were put to their new use, suggests that the Muslims' zeal did not extend to a rigorous respect for the religious injunction which forbids figurative representation. The columns were redeployed without being disfigured, and their Hindu motifs were accepted into the Islamic scheme. So here, at its very inception, the tone is set for the ensuing tradition of Islamic

Columns in the cloister of the Qutb mosque.

building in India: by one means or another (for the use of previously existing fragments was only one means) Hindu forms entered the Islamic architectural vocabulary. To the Muslims, the columns' only unsatisfactory feature was their shortness: the builders had to place one on top of another to give the cloister the desired height.

Another way in which Hindu ideas were incorporated is revealed by the mosque's screen, to the west of the courtyard. At first sight this elegant arcade of five pointed arches seems the purest statement of Islamic civilization. In general, the curved shape of an arch arises from the method of constructing with radiating voussoirs. But a close examination of the construction of these arches reveals that they are not fully true arches: each is composed not of a fan of voussoirs (like the arch of a humpback bridge) but rather of piles of horizontal courses with each course slightly overlapping the one below (like two stepped piles of books leaning towards each other). The arched shape has been achieved by carving off the ends of these courses; only at the very top of each arch are voussoirs used. This is a sure sign that for the construction of the screen, Qutb-ud-din relied not on imported Muslim builders (who would have been perfectly familiar with the principle of the true arch) but on local Hindu builders (who generally used the less efficient step or corbelling method). The form of the arches is Islamic, but the technology is largely Hindu. Hindu ideas have entered an Islamic building, in this case, through the employment of indigenous craftsmen.

The same process is revealed again in the decorative carving on the piers between the screen's arches. The basis of the scheme is Islamic, consisting of Koranic inscriptions interwoven with arabesques, but the convoluted and exuberant foliage betrays the hand of the Hindu craftsman, who has adapted skills otherwise applied to temple decoration. The two elements are combined in a glorious syncretism, to produce one of the finest passages of architectural decoration in India. That work should be lavished on the screen is appropriate, for, as in all Indian mosques, the screen is the most conspicuous feature: it served as the front and entrance to the prayer hall — the mosque's main enclosed space (now ruined).

Immediately in front of the screen stands an iron column. This forms no part of the religious scheme: it is there purely for

Carving on the screen of the Qutb mosque.

its antique value. As far as the inscriptions on it can be decipered and interpreted, it appears that it is a standard of the Hindu god Vishnu, wrought in the fourth century, probably at the command of the emperor of Bihar, Chandragupta II. Its precise original location is disputed, but it is believed that it was brought to Delhi by the Tomar Rajputs. It was incorporated into the mosque presumably because the early Muslims were impressed — as are modern visitors — that in the course of its exceptionally long life it has not succumbed to rust.

Towering above the cloister of this central courtyard (though standing outside it) is the vast **Qutb Minar**. A minar (like its smaller relation, the minaret) is a tower appended to a mosque, from which the muezzin calls the faithful to prayer. This one is as much symbolic as functional: any muezzin who climbed to its highest balcony would be rewarded with a fine view but would not be heard. It was built primarily as a victory tower — an unambiguous demonstration of the power of Islam. Qutb-ud-din's own name means 'axis of the faith', and so by calling the tower 'Qutb Minar' he honoured himself and stressed its symbolic role as an axis of Islamic dominion. In defiance of this symbolism, perhaps, there arose the myth that the tower was originally a Hindu structure, built by the Rajput kings. This theory — still occasionally heard locally — is quite without basis: clearly Hindu masons worked on the construction, but the conception is Islamic. The design is based closely on Afghan prototypes, from which the angular flanges are derived. Each of the balconies is supported on a web of tiny arches — a structural form called *muqarnas* which was common in Persia under the Seljuks.

The tower's five storeys together reach a height of 72.5 m (238 ft). The height is emphasized by a pronounced taper, from a base diameter of 14 m (47 ft) to a diameter at the top of just over 2.7 m (9 ft): this taper exaggerates the effects of perspective, making the diminished top seem even further away than it is in fact. From inscriptions within the tower, it appears that its construction was the result of combined effort. When Qutb-ud-din died in 1210, only the first storey had been completed, and the construction of a further three storeys was overseen by his son-in-law and successor, Shams-ud-din Iltutmish (r. 1211–36). In this state it was apparently considered complete, but when the top (or fourth) storey was damaged by lightning in the mid-14th century, it was replaced by two storeys; these increased the overall height and introduced white marble into the previously exclusively red sandstone scheme.

Not content with completing his father-in-law's tower, Iltutmish also enlarged the mosque. He did this by extending the screen at both ends, beyond the cloister, and erecting an outer cloister which enclosed the whole of the original mosque. This in effect created two new courtyards flanking the original one, and brought the Qutb Minar within the main mosque area.

A later Sultan of Delhi, the third main contributor to this group of buildings, Ala-ud-din Khalji (r. 1296–1316), had even more grandiose designs. He planned to repeat Iltutmish's operation by again doubling the length of the screen and building a third enclosing cloister which would dwarf his precedessors' courtyards. He also planned a second tower, to have twice the base area and rise to twice the height of the Qutb Minar. In this ambition (as in one or two others) Ala-ud-din overreached himself: the rough, unfinished stump of the **Alai Minar** stands to the north of the mosque, a frustrated tower of Babel.

Ala-ud-din did succeed, however, in extending the area of the mosque, adding a further courtyard to the east of the previously existing group of three. (The visitor without a compass may orient himself at any time if he remembers that by standing in the central courtyard and facing the screen, he would be doing what the builders intended the faithful to do, namely facing Mecca — that is westwards, in Indian mosques.)

The masons responsible for the construction of Iltutmish's and Ala-ud-din's extensions appear to have been anxious to preserve the stylistic unity of the whole. When they constructed the outer cloister, they did not have at their disposal a further supply of Hindu temple columns, and so in order to match the columns of the inner cloister they carved new, imitation temple columns. Though building a mosque, they carved columns in a Hindu rather than an Islamic form, to be consistent with the earlier part, assembled from Hindu fragments: integrity of style seemingly counted for more than religious association. The arrangement of the outer cloisters echoes that of the old, inner one even to the detail that the columns are raised one above another in two tiers. The later builders, in other words, deliberately repeated the arrange- ment which the earlier builders had adopted by necessity. The imitation columns are much less richly decorated than the genuine ones. Their plainness is evidently due not to a Muslim objection to Hindu decoration, since this would have applied equally to the original columns; more probably, it is due to a desire to build swiftly and economically.

In a section of the cloister added by Ala-ud-din (imme- diately to the south-east of the Qutb Minar) he built also a gateway, to serve as an entrance into his vast projected court. This gate, known as the **Alai Darwaza**, was com- pleted in 1311. It consists of a square chamber, richly decorated with relief carving and surmounted by a dome. The exterior face, with its high entrance arch flanked by recesses and screened windows, is one of the best resolved compositions in early Indo-Islamic architecture. The striking juxtaposition of red sandstone and white marble (later to become a favourite device) here makes its debut.

Few archaeological sites in India are straightforward: they rarely contain single, isolated monuments, and usually include a number of more or less related buildings which might cover an enormous time-span. The Qutb complex is no exception: apart from the mosque and its adjuncts already described, there are numerous other structures nearby. Of these, two tombs deserve special mention. Close by the Alai Darwaza is the small, domed **Tomb of Imam**

The Alai Darwaza in the Qutb mosque.

Zamin, a Turkestani saint. He came to India in about 1500 and fulfilled some office in relation to the Qutb mosque; accordingly he built his own tomb there, in which he was buried in 1538. It is a sandstone structure with fine perforated screens or *jalis*; some parts are covered with the highly polished white plaster known as *chunam*. As usual in such tombs, the dome rests on an octagonal base, which is made by cutting off the corners of the square space at ceiling level. But while in most Delhi tombs, the corners are cut off by arches or squinches, here flat beams are used. This arrangement is more typical of tombs in Gujarat; and the use of *jali* screens was also commoner there than in Delhi at this period. (One other contemporary tomb in Delhi shares this combination of Gujarati features: the tomb of Shaikh Yusuf Qattal in Malaviyanagar district.)

The **Tomb of Iltutmish**, built in 1235 shortly before that sultan's death, is situated just outside his own extension to the mosque, at the north-west corner behind the screen. The cenotaph stands in the centre of the tomb chamber, of which the dome — constructed on Hindu rather than Islamic principles — has collapsed. The decorative carving of the chamber is exceptionally lavish; executed in red standstone, it incorporates a number of traditional Hindu motifs (such as lotus flowers and bells on chains) as well as Islamic inscriptions. On the west side are three ornate *mihrab* recesses, which indicate the direction of Mecca.

The dignity and refinement of all these buildings should not lead us to misjudge the personalities of the early Delhi Sultans: they were as ruthless and despotic as their age expected. Qutb-ud-din, the true founder of the sultanate, though capable of generosity, prudently balanced that capacity with ferociousness. His sultanate was not founded wholly on enlightened liberalism. As a contemporary court historian admiringly said, 'his gifts were bestowed by hundreds of thousands, and his slaughters likewise were by hundreds of thousands'.

MEHRAULI

The district of Mehrauli, around the Qutb complex, contains a number of interesting monuments, including some of the Mughal period. In the area of rough ground to the west of the road which leads south from the complex, stand two early Mughal mosques. The first of these, the **Madhi Masjid**, is of a most unusual form. A mosque of standard pattern has a continuous covered hall or sanctuary bordering the western side of the courtyard; sometimes a more basic type is found, which has no hall but only a simple wall to denote the direction of prayer. In the Madhi Masjid these two types are combined: the central section of the western range is a simple wall-mosque, but this is flanked by covered halls. The result is that the range has a greater variety than usual, but it has little coherence; evidently the builders did not consider their experiment a success, for it was not repeated. More satisfactory are the brilliant blue tiles which run in a line across the façades. The courtyard is raised on an artificial terrace, and is enclosed by a strong wall with corner turrets so that the whole mosque is turned into a miniature fort. It is entered through an impressive gateway, with balcony windows in the trabeate Hindu style. The gateway closely resembles the tombs built in the period of the Lodi sultans, who preceded the Mughals, and the arches of the sanctuary are also of a Lodi type. The precise date of this mosque is not known, but if it is indeed Mughal then it must be one of the earliest buildings constructed by that dynasty, and indicates the stylistic continuity between the Mughals and their predecessors.

A few hundred yards to the north is the **Jamali Kamali Masjid**. 'Jamali' was the pseudonym of a poet and saint who flourished at the early Mughal court, and who built this mosque. As is commonly the case with such private commissions, the patron's tomb stands in an adjacent compound: it

The Jamali Kamali Masjid.

consists of a single, domed, square chamber, decorated inside with coloured tiles and painted plaster-work. Jamali died in 1535 and was buried along with an unidentified companion (indicated by the pseudonym 'Kamali'). The mosque, constructed between 1528 and 1536, represents another step forward from the Madhi Masjid towards the distinct Mughal style. It is somewhat more refined and better proportioned; still robust but no longer so heavy, it lacks the awkwardness of its older neighbour. And with its red sandstone facing, relieved by white detailing, its colouring is typically Mughal: this combination, of course, had long been in use (it is found, for example, in the Alai Darwaza of the Qutb mosque) but it had been less favoured in the Lodi period; the Mughals revived it, and used it so repeatedly that it is almost a hallmark of their early style. The main façade is enriched by some delicately carved details, such as the rosettes in the spandrels of the arches, and the fringe of buds on the intrados of the central arch; but these decorations are sparse, so that the general effect is still severe.

Slightly to the west of the Qutb complex, on the edge of Mehrauli village itself, is the **Tomb of Adham Khan**. The principal occupant was the son of Maham Anga, a woman who had served as one of Akbar's wet nurses. This quasi-relationship customarily gave an opportunity for promotion, and Adham Khan was at first successful. But he quarrelled

Adham Khan's tomb.

with the husband of another of the emperor's former wet nurses: growing jealous of the trust and favour his rival enjoyed, he murdered him in 1562. This was the occasion on which Akbar helped to establish his reputation for fearlessness, by disarming the assassin, though barehanded himself. While still dazed from Akbar's blow, Adham Khan was thrown from the fort ramparts. His mother died soon after, reportedly of grief. At this, sentiment reasserted itself in Akbar, and he constructed the tomb in memory of both mother and son. Its octagonal form, with a veranda of pointed arches, follows a pattern of tomb design which had been developed early in the 15th century, under the Sayyid sultans — again demonstrating how architectural traditions could continue irrespective of a change of dynasty. But it is larger than its antecedents, and its pomposity is further enhanced by the commanding position, for it stands on part of the walls of the ancient Rajput fortress, Lal Kot. The complicated system of staircases concealed within its walls has earned it the local name, Bul-bulaiyan (or 'maze').

Also in the vicinity of Mehrauli is one of the last Mughal structures, the gateway to a palace known as the **Zafar Mahal**, built by the emperor Bahadur Shah Zafar, in about 1850. A huge central arch is flanked by smaller openings in several storeys; this composition and the colour scheme are both revivals of early Mughal ideas, and the gateway recaptures something of the former grandeur; but the carved details are weak and shallow, and thus typical of the phase of decline.

At the eastern edge of Delhi, between the ring road and the Jumna, lies the impressive fort known as the **Purana Qila** (or 'old fort'). The ancient mound which it encloses is the site identified by some archaeologists as the Indraprastha of the *Mahabharata*, but the surviving structures date from a much later period: they are the work jointly of Humayun, the second Mughal emperor (r. 1530–56), and the Sur sultans who temporarily deposed him (1540–55). The first Mughal emperor, Babur, had had comparatively little opportunity for great building projects: during his short reign in India (1526–30) he constructed numerous gardens (to satisfy his leading passion) and some minor buildings, but he produced no ambitious and durable works. Much of the time he

THE PURANA QILA

seemingly preferred to live in tents. It was therefore his successor, Humayun, who laid the foundations of this first Mughal capital city — the sixth of the seven Islamic Delhis. He began the construction of the fort, originally called Dinpannah ('asylum of the faith'). Humayun's loss of the Delhi throne in 1540 to Sher Shah Sur did not interrupt the building programme, and indeed the only two surviving buildings within the fort were constructed by Sher Shah whilst Humayun was in exile, and were later used by Humayun after his victorious return in 1555.

The fort wall, completed by Sher Shah, is more than one and a half kilometres (1 mile) long, and is punctuated by three gates, of which the western one is now used as the main entrance. Sher Shah's two buildings stand close by inside this gate: they are a graceful mosque, known as the **Qala-i-Kuhna Masjid**, and a three-storey octagonal pavilion, known as the **Sher Mandal**. Belying the political instability of the age in which they were produced, the designs of these buildings are confident and resolved. Stylistically they are based on earlier sultanate buildings; and yet at the same time they look forward to some of Akbar's period, especially in their simple, geometrical plans, the harmonious proportions of their massing, and their clean, uncluttered lines. It is ironic that the inception of the Mughal style was achieved here, in buildings erected under the patronage of the Mughals' early rivals.

One aspect of their derivation from earlier sultanate architecture is the considerable dependence on that most essentially Islamic form, the pointed arch. The red and white colour scheme also recalls Indo-Islamic precedent; even the

The western gate of the Purana Qila.

The Sher Mandal.

introduction of a grey-blue stone in the spandrels of the lower arch of the fort gate has a precedent, in tombs of the Lodi period such as the Bara Gumbad in Delhi (*c*. 1500). And again like earlier Indo-Islamic buildings, these incorporate certain forms of Hindu origin: notable here are the *jarokhas*, or small, projecting balconies supported on corbels (on the gate and the mosque); the *chajjas*, or deep, slanting dripstones in place of eaves (on the front of the mosque and on the Sher Mandal); and the *chattris*, or domed, octagonal kiosks (crowning the gate and the Sher Mandal). The octagonal towers at the rear of the mosque have, on their lower storeys, arches of the traditional Hindu stepped form.

Built in 1541, the mosque marks a further step in the process of refinement and elaboration noted in the Jamali Kamali Masjid. The basic elements and composition are the same as in that earlier example, but this design is more adventurous. On the screen of the sanctuary, each of the entrance arches is framed within a higher, stilted arch; and the repetition of this strong form, together with the variety in the arches' sizes, establishes an agitated rhythm. This rhythm is overlaid by delicate carved and coloured decoration, the mosaic in the tympanum over the central arch being particularly fine.

The fort must once have contained many more buildings for the use of Sher Shah's court, but only the mosque and the Sher Mandal have survived. Both these buildings are in a tolerable state of preservation, though the Sher Mandal has

The Qala-i-Kuhna
Masjid in the Purana
Qila.

The rear wall of the
Qala-i-Kuhna Masjid.

lost much of the white inlay decoration which originally
lightened its red bulk, and the courtyard of the mosque has
been converted into a garden.

The two rulers responsible for this fort and its buildings
were markedly different in temperament. Humayun inherited
the kingdom of his father, but sadly few of that intellectual
adventurer's qualities. He was obsessed with astrology, and
not only did this superstition affect his judgement, but he
allowed it to direct the administration: he would attend to
matters of a given kind only on a day governed by an
appropriately symbolic planet. This system did not make for
efficient and sound rule. Sher Shah, by comparison, did not
have Humayun's advantages of birth, but made up for this
by his determination and pragmatism. Of Afghan descent,
his grandfather had come to India to take service under the
Delhi Sultans, but the ambitious Sher Shah was not satsified
with service and carved out his own sultanate in eastern
India. The weakness of Mughal power (occasioned partly by
Humayun's eccentricity and partly by the disloyalty of his
brothers) gave Sher Shah an opportunity for a still greater
prize, and in 1540 he took it: a brief and tidy campaign
made him Sultan of Delhi.

After a period spent wandering about the Rajasthan
desert, hoping for a change of fortune, Humayun abandoned his Indian inheritance and sought the protection of
the Shah of Persia. The Shah at first welcomed his guest, no
doubt encouraged by Humayun's gift to him of India's
famous diamond, the Koh-i-Noor. But eventually he
demanded a higher price for the asylum he offered: he

required Humayun to convert from the Sunni faith of his ancestors to the Shia faith of his host. The doctrinal schism within Islam had occurred shortly after the death of the Prophet, the issue being who was to be considered his legitimate successor as Caliph (the Sunnis insisting that the Caliph is elected, the Shias believing that succession should be restricted to descendants of the Prophet through his son-in-law). The majority of Indian Muslims were (and still are) Sunni, and so Humayun's reluctant conversion created a potential problem in the event of his recapture of India.

Whilst Humayun was tormented with this dilemma in Persia, Sher Shah, in India, was sweeping aside Humayun's astrological conceits and establishing sound systems of government. His programme of road building, to connect the major cities of northern India, and his system of land revenue were among the measures which anticipated (and facilitated) the great reforms of Akbar's reign. The Sur dynasty would no doubt have achieved much more if its founder had lived longer, but Sher Shah died in 1545, to be succeeded by his less resolute son, Islam Shah (r. 1545–54). Islam Shah was to Sher Shah what Humayun was to Babur, and the fortunes of the Sur dynasty now repeated the pattern of the early Mughals: the determined father had won an empire, only to die after a few years; the less able son kept it for ten years only to see his grip on it loosen. Both Mughals and Surs had been short-lived dynasties. We would perhaps now hear little of either were it not that the contention for the throne following the death of Islam Shah returned it eventually to Humayun's hands, and the Mughals' second coming was more lasting.

After his recapture of the Delhi throne and his Indian empire, in June 1555, Humayun had little opportunity to inflict further harm on the administration, for he died a few months later. The very manner of his death was typical of this pious, bookish man. Inheriting Sher Shah's fine embellishments to his fort, Humayun used the Sher Mandal as a library. On 24 January 1556 he was standing on the roof of this pavilion, about to descend the stone staircase to cross over to the mosque for prayer, when he heard the call of the muezzin. He turned to bow in respect, lost his balance and fell down the stairs. He died of his injuries a few days later.

To the west of the Purana Qila, on the other side of the main road, is an imposing gateway — one of the few

Detail of the Khair-ul Manazil Masjid.

surviving fragments of the city wall which Sher Shah built around Delhi in the 1540s. Adjacent, to its south, are a small mosque called the **Khair-ul Manazil Masjid** and a *madrasa* (or religious college) which were built in 1561 by Maham Anga, the mother of Adham Khan (see p. 36). The facings of these buildings are gone, so that their rubble construction is revealed. The *madrasa* was the scene of an attempt against Akbar's life: the slave of a disgraced courtier fired an arrow from its roof and succeeded in grazing the emperor, but, in the words of a contemporary account, 'the attendants of the emperor instantly fell upon the traitor and, with strokes of sword and dagger, they sent him to hell'.

HUMAYUN'S TOMB

The custom among Muslim rulers and dignitaries in India was to build one's tomb during one's lifetime, but Humayun's accidental death, following so soon after the wilderness years, found him unprepared, and it was some years later that he was finally laid to rest in the handsome structure which lies to the south of the Purana Qila, east of the Mathura road.

Something of the character of Humayun, his career and the manner of his death were described in the preceding section; it should in fairness be added that the apparent failure in his career was partly due to jealous brothers, who impeded his resistance to Sher Shah Sur. While Humayun was campaigning against Sher Shah, one brother, Hindal, took advantage of his absence from the centre to declare himself emperor. And even when he had been deposed by Sher Shah, the other brothers, Askari and Kamran, in control respectively of Kandahar and Kabul, refused to give him quarter. Humayun's recapture of those two cities, in 1545, marked a turning point in his fortunes, though it was another ten years before he re-won India, and the ousted brothers continued to plague him. They had been able to do so for so long because Humayun repeatedly let pass opportunities to suppress them decisively — to the frustration of his advisers; but eventually he was persuaded to banish Askari and have the more persistent Kamran blinded and sent on pilgrimage to Mecca (from which he did not return). Humayun's capacity for fraternal forgiveness — quite undeserved by his fickle brothers — has earned him, among historians, a reputation for sentimentality; but it also makes him likeable,

42

Humayun's tomb.

when compared with the quick temper common to many of his contemporaries.

His tomb, built in the 1560s, was commissioned by his senior widow, known as Haji Begam, who brought from Persia for the purpose an architect named Mirak Mirza Ghiyas. It inaugurates a sequence of grand Mughal tombs: indeed tombs became a speciality of the Mughal school in spite of the religious injunction forbidding pretentious mausolea. Humayun's was the first in the sequence because his father, the founding emperor, Babur, had expressed an orthodox wish that nothing should cover his grave: he was buried initially in a garden in Agra, and later transferred (again in accordance with a wish expressed before he died) to a grave in Kabul.

The essential design ingredients of Humayun's tomb are derived from those of earlier Delhi sultans. The use of the octagon in planning, and the prominent *iwans* — the high arches in the centres of the façades — are both features which are found in tombs of the 15th-century Sayyid and

N

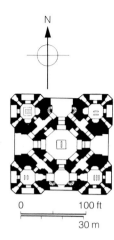

0   100 ft

30 m

The ground floor of
Humayun's tomb.

Lodi sultans of Delhi. These traditional features, however, are here combined on an unprecedented, massive scale, and with a new vigour. Especially satisfying is the depth of the composition. The position of the frame surrounding each *iwan* — set back slightly from the rest of the façade — together with the chamfering of the corners, gives depth and movement. And these already varied surfaces are punctured by large arched recesses, which in turn contain further openings; and yet the voids are held in balance by the solid parts. The lines are clear but restless: the decorative border along the roof-line, in negotiating the *iwans*, takes a complicated course over the varied geometrical solids. This richness in the geometrical structure is complemented by the surface decoration — the flat parts of the façades are divided into panels of assorted sizes, symmetrically grouped to fill the spaces. This kind of treatment is very common in Mughal architecture; here, it is greatly emphasized by the use of three different coloured stones.

Internally, the tomb consists of a central, octagonal hall which rises through two storeys, and is surrounded by smaller octagonal chambers. The main sarcophagus stands in the central hall, oriented — in accordance with Muslim practice — on the north-south axis (the body is traditionally placed with the head to the north, the face turned sideways towards Mecca). Major tombs are sometimes accompanied by a mosque; but otherwise the western side of the tomb itself is generally provided not with an open doorway like the other sides, but with a solid wall containing a *mihrab*, or arched recess, as in the *qibla* wall of a mosque. This blocking of the western side often disrupts the symmetry and restricts the flow of light. The builders of Humayun's tomb were evidently reluctant to conform to the practice. Every side of the central hall here has a *jali* (pierced screen) through which the light filters; but it may be noticed that on the western side, the outline of a *mihrab* is superimposed over the *jali* — so that religious convention is obeyed without detriment to the design.

The general effect of the central hall is now a little spartan, but originally it was softened by furnishings. The English merchant William Finch visited the building in 1611 and described it as

> spread with rich carpets, the tombe itself covered with a pure white sheet, a rich semiane [coloured tent] over head, and in

44

front certaine bookes on small tressels, by which stand his sword, tucke [turban] and shooes.

In the surrounding chambers are many lesser sarcophagi, added later; their occupants have not been identified individually, though it is known that they include wives of Humayun and a number of later Mughal emperors and princes — so that the individual's tomb became almost a family one. The sex of the occupant of a sarcophagus is indicated by a simple symbolism: a box for writing implements carved on the top indicates a male, a writing slate a female. In 1857, the tomb was the scene of the final demise of the Mughal dynasty: the last emperor, Bahadur Shah II, sought sanctuary in the tomb of his ancestor when the mutiny collapsed, before he was arrested by the British.

The tomb stands in the centre of a large, walled garden, entered through two gates: a principal one to the south (now closed) and a lesser one to the west (now generally used). The garden is divided into four parterres by water-courses, an arrangement based on the Persian *charbagh* (or 'four-

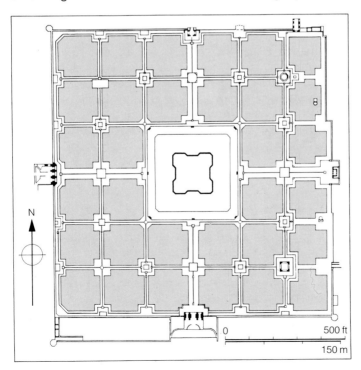

The garden of Humayun's tomb.

fold garden'). Both in the combining of tomb and garden into a single ensemble, and to some degree in the plan and overall form of the building itself, Humayun's tomb anticipates the Taj Mahal.

The central dome has a double shell: an outer shell to achieve height on the exterior, and a shallow inner shell to conceal the great void in the interior. Like the garden plan, this device was developed in Persia. Such features are sometimes cited as aspects of the tomb's supposedly Persian character, which is considered the result of the employment of a Persian architect. This analysis is misleading: it should not be supposed that Mirak Mirza Ghiyas was introducing into India ideas not seen there before. Though Persian in origin, both features have precedents in India: Babur had built *charbagh* gardens there, and the tomb of Sikander Lodi in Delhi (1517) has a double-shell dome. Persia, to be sure, was the main source of Islamic design, and if all that is meant by calling Humayun's tomb Persian is that it is Islamic, then the description is just; but it would still be misleading, for India had its own Islamic tradition, originally derived from Persia certainly, but developing differently. The Mughals occasionally (as in this case) looked to Persia for fresh talent, but their architecture was fundamentally a development of that of the earlier Delhi Sultans. This tomb's dependence on that local tradition — its derivation from earlier tombs in the city — has already been outlined; its immediate progenitors are not Persian but Indian.

It is an aspect of the separate development that Islamic buildings in India, unlike those in Persia, drew part of their inspiration from Hindu traditions. The Hindu motifs that most commonly occur in them — and that were noted in the buildings in the Purana Qila — are the *chajja* (dripstone), simplified temple columns, brackets and corbels, and two complex forms which are made up of these details — the *chattri* (domed kiosk) and the *jarokha* (balcony window). All these forms and motifs had been developed in Indian medieval temples, but that they later entered the standard repertoire of Indo-Islamic architecture. In Humayun's tomb — the present example — Hindu *chattris*, complete with temple columns and *chajjas*, surround the central dome. Also Hindu are the bulbous finial surmounting the dome, and the star motif in the spandrels of the main arches. These details do not hide the building's essentially Islamic character, but they qualify it sufficiently to distinguish the tomb from Islamic buildings in other countries.

Humayun's tomb is attended by a host of lesser monuments. To its south-east, within the garden, stands a small, square-planned tomb, datable to 1590 (see the illustration on p. 21); its occupant is unidentified, though its popular designation — **'the Barber's Tomb'** — suggests it may commemorate a favourite servant of the emperor. Immediately outside the garden's western gate, to the left as one leaves, is a wall of the so-called **Arab Sarai**. This is a spacious enclosure, believed to have been built to house the masons who worked on Humayun's tomb; it can be entered by the impressive gate at the far end of the wall (or by another on its eastern side). Within the Sarai, on a plinth, stand the dilapidated **Afsarwala Mosque and Tomb**, built by an officer of Akbar's in 1566. All these buildings are typical of the early Mughal period: each is a bold composition of arches and niches of various sizes — a pattern made more dramatic by the red and white colour scheme, and slightly relieved by patches of carved or coloured ornament. The style is more elegant than that typical of the preceding Lodi period: the forms are less heavy and the stone is more crisply cut; but it retains an element of the former severity.

Adjacent to the Arab Sarai's northern gate and at right angles to it (and so facing the western gate to Humayun's tomb) is another gate. This was the entrance to a space known as **Bu Halima's Garden**, which lies beyond it, to the west. Though they are of obscure origin, the gate and the garden apparently existed before Humayun's tomb was built; the greater tomb complex was, however, built on the axis which they had established, and so incorporated them into the larger scheme: Bu Halima's garden became a sort of

The Afsarwala mosque and tomb.

subsidiary court to the tomb garden. (The Archaeological Survey has followed the spirit of this adaptation by housing the ticket office for the tomb in Bu Halima's gate.)

To the south of what remains of Bu Halima's garden is another enclosure. This contains the **Mosque and Tomb of Isa Khan**, a nobleman at the time of the Sur interregnum. The small mosque, with its three-arched screen, is similar to the nearby Afsarwala mosque, though earlier in date and weaker in design: in the Afsarwala mosque the three arches relate in a single composition; here they are comparatively small and dispersed, and the screen derives its effect less from its form than from the brashly coloured tile-work. The adjacent tomb, though built in 1547, revives the style of the 15th-century tombs of the Sayyid sultans (as Adham Khan's tomb was to do again, a little later): the octagonal chamber is surrounded by a deep veranda, and the rather squat dome is surrounded by small *chattris*. In this tomb, as in its 15th-century prototypes, are found some of the basic ingredients of the later design of Humayun's tomb, but combined more crudely, without the refined finish and balanced proportions of the Mughal building. Isa Khan's tomb also prefigures Humayun's tomb in being contained in a walled compound: this arrangement derives from an earlier tradition of fortified tombs — typified, for example, by the tombs of Sultan Ghari (1231), Ghiyas-ud-din Tughluq (1320) and Sikander Lodi (1517); but Isa Khan's tomb marks the point of transition between this early fortified type and the tomb in a spacious garden — a pattern much loved by the Mughals, and properly inaugurated in Humayun's tomb.

Finally in this area, are two more tombs which, though similar to each other, are otherwise unusual in design. One is the **Nila Gumbad**, which stands just outside the eastern wall of the garden of Humayun's tomb; the other is the **Sabz Burj**, which stands rather uncomfortably in the centre of the roundabout on the Mathura road, near the entrance to the area. The occupants cannot be identified with certainty, though they were probably noblemen in the early Mughal period. The buildings' names (meaning 'blue dome' and 'green tower') simply describe the decoration. Both tombs have brilliant glazed tiles covering the domes (those on the Sabz Burj are modern replicas of the original ones), besides some other coloured tile-work on the drums or façades. The patterns of these tiles are not like those on other Indian

The Nila Gumbad.

buildings, and indeed the tombs as a whole have a curiously foreign appearance; they are among the very few buildings in the country which could fairly be described as Persian in character, because they lack those features, such as *chattris* and *chajjas*, which mark the separate development of the Islamic tradition in India.

Opposite the area of Humayun's tomb, on the western side of the Mathura road, is the district of Nizamuddin. An ancient Muslim quarter clustered around the tomb of a saint, this district survives as an urban village, an enclave which is scarcely affected by or even connected to the changing metropolis which surrounds it. At its centre, within a walled compound approached through winding lanes and covered passages, stands the *dargah* or tomb of the saint, Shaikh Nizam-ud-din. The saint lived from 1236 to 1325 and exerted a considerable influence over some of the Delhi sultans of his times. From zeal and respect, his tomb has often been rebuilt; the basis of the present structure was built during the reign of Akbar, in 1562, but even this late work is hidden under the florid accretions of later centuries. It is still an object of veneration to pilgrims who come in large numbers, who form a perpetual busy crowd around the tomb, and whose offerings pay for its further embellishment in the taste of the day. Consequently, the *dargah* is of little interest to the antiquarian, but it provides a living example of how such places are used, developed and administered. The people and the purpose are of more interest than the edifice, for its antique value is lost through their survival.

The tomb is hemmed in by other buildings. It stands in the courtyard of a large mosque, built in the year of the saint's death. The mosque sanctuary is of a simple and severe form, somewhat obscured by patches of green paint. Abutting the courtyard to the south are a number of smaller tombs, including that of Amir Khusrau, a poet and disciple of the saint, and that of Jahanara, a daughter of Shah Jahan. Just outside the *dargah* enclosure, concealed in an almost inaccessible corner, is the gem-like **Tomb of Ataga Khan**. Though small, it is covered with intricate mosaic and carved relief, making it more like a casket than a building; the patterns are mostly geometric, complementing the larger geometry of the structural form, and adding dashes of

NIZAMUDDIN

Ataga Khan's tomb, Nizamuddin.

The Chaunsath
Khamba.

brilliant colour to the red and white frame. Ataga Khan, who was the husband of one of Akbar's former wet nurses, was one of the emperor's ministers and the victim of Adham Khan's assassination plot in 1562. His tomb was completed in 1566.

Close by to the east is the **Chaunsath Khamba**, a pavilion supported (as its name implies) on sixty-four columns, and containing a number of individual graves. It was built in 1623, during the reign of Jahangir. The exclusive use of white marble prefigures the architecture of Shah Jahan's reign, but the forms have a clarity of line typical of the earlier period: the arches, for example, are pointed not cusped. The openings are blocked by *jalis*, divided by heavy mullions and transoms, in the Gujarati style.

The **Tomb of Abdur Rahim Khan**, also known as Khan-i-Khanan, stands just outside Nizamuddin, on the opposite side of the main road. The nobleman buried here was the son of Bairam Khan, the able and trustworthy commander who had protected Akbar during his minority. Khan-i-Khanan also served Akbar, and later Jahangir. But both father and son were victims of the changeable political climate in which they worked. Akbar's very succession had depended on Bairam Khan, who defeated the other contenders in the name of his teenage master; but as Akbar's self-confidence grew, he found such faithful protection irksome, and Bairam Khan was dropped. Similarly, after long service, Khan-i-Khanan quarrelled with Jahangir, and spent some time in prison before his death in 1626. The design of his tomb is clearly derived from that of Humayun's tomb, and it marks another step in the development of the tradition towards its apogee in the Taj Mahal. The overall form is here more compact than in Humayun's tomb — the plan is not a congregation of octagons but a square (the plan of the Taj Mahal was later to combine both shapes, being a square with its corners cut off, and thus an irregular octagon). Khan-i-Khanan's tomb is also more compact through having its water channels and pools on the podium rather than in a spacious garden. The tomb is badly damaged: some of its stone facing, including all of the marble from the dome, was removed to be used in other buildings; consequently it has lost much of its splendour and receives little of the attention due to such a successful and influential design experiment.

Before the Mughal invasion, the capital of India's northern Muslim sultanate had always been Delhi; and throughout the reigns of Babur and Humayun, through the Sur interregnum, and for the first few years of Akbar's reign, Delhi continued in this pre-eminent role. But Akbar removed his court 160 km (100 miles) south, to Agra. In the following eighty years, the seat of power was moved many times again, to various cities including Fatehpur Sikri and Lahore, but in time it always returned to Agra, which never lost its importance. In 1638, however, Shah Jahan decided to abandon Agra finally, and construct a new capital on the ancient site of Delhi. The move was largely a matter of prestige: it provided this most ambitious of Mughal builders with an opportunity to construct a city which would be exclusively his own, owing nothing to his forbears, yet sharing in the long-established distinction of Delhi. His new city, the seventh Muslim city on the site, was built slightly to the north of its predecessors, on the bank of the Jumna, and was named after himself, Shahjahanabad (though it is now commonly known as Old Delhi).

Building operations began in 1638 and were largely complete when the court was finally transferred to its new quarters ten years later. The city was encompassed by a fortification wall, which was originally pierced by fourteen major gates. Among the surviving gates are three on the southern side — known as the Delhi, Turkoman and Ajmeri gates; these are all simple in form and rugged in style, and thus unusual for their period, suggesting a degree of haste in their construction.

Apart from the city wall, imperial patronage was responsible also for the city's principal streets and mosques. The street plan was dominated by two major routes: **Chandni Chowk**, which crosses the centre of the city from west to east, and **Faiz Bazar**, which runs southwards from the fort. Both are long, straight and impressively broad. They were originally lined with shops, whose roofs formed terraces from which the public could view processions; and in the centre of each street flowed an elegant canal. Apart from being routes and bazaars, these two streets acted as breathing spaces in the mostly dense urban structure, for all of the other streets were winding and narrow. Not many of the city's original domestic and commercial buildings now survive;

very few substantial houses date from before the 19th century, and most are modern. But in spite of the rebuilding, the original street pattern has been largely maintained. So too has the basis of the city's social organization, which followed the traditional Indian system, with people inhabiting districts (or *mohallas*) according to their caste and profession. Consequently, Shahjahanabad today still has the atmosphere and appearance — even if it has lost the fabric — of an old city.

In the angle between the two main streets, to the south of Chandni Chowk, stands the city's principal mosque, the **Jami Masjid**. Taking advantage of a natural outcrop of rock, the mosque has a commanding position, and its dignity is greatly enhanced by the flights of steps required to reach its courtyard. It was begun by Shah Jahan in 1650; five thousand masons worked daily on its construction for six years, at a cost of a million rupees. With a courtyard measuring over 91 m (300 ft) across, it is one of the largest mosques in India. As the name Jami denotes, its principal function was as a congregational or Friday mosque,

The Jami Masjid of Delhi.

intended to accommodate the entire population when gathered for the Friday prayer. It was also important as a social and commercial centre: the 19th-century writer Ahmad Khan Saiyid, records that even in his time the mosque's outer steps were cluttered by a daily market, where one could buy horses, birds and cloth or be entertained by jugglers and story-tellers. And it was also an imperial stage, where the emperor could be seen attending the Friday prayer: the French traveller François Bernier described how, during the reign of Shah Jahan's son Aurangzeb, the streets of the city were watered, to settle the dust in preparation for the emperor's weekly journey to the mosque — a journey which he made sometimes on a caparisoned elephant 'and sometimes in a throne gleaming with azure and gold, placed on a litter covered with scarlet or brocade, which eight chosen men, in handsome attire, carry on their shoulders'.

Such splendid props formed a suitable complement to the architectural setting, one of the most noble and magnificent of Mughal compositions. The screen of the sanctuary contains eleven cusped arches — an arcade of five on either side of the massive central *iwan*. Above them rise three bulbous domes, each decorated with restrained vertical black stripes which emphasize their undulating contours. The placing of the minarets was a perennial problem in the design of mosques; here they are integrated into the ends of the screen, to frame the composition and balance the pinnacles which flank the *iwan*. This solution had been tried before, but never with such success, and from this point on it became standard practice in Mughal mosques. The design does not, however, solve the other and more intractable problem, that a lofty *iwan* tends to obscure the central dome; here, the power of the dome has been sacrificed to achieve a grander gesture in the screen.

That sacrifice was perhaps encouraged by the role of the *iwan* as a focus for those at prayer in the courtyard. The only liturgically essential part of a mosque is the *qibla* wall, the back wall of the sanctuary; by facing this, the worshipper faces westwards, that is towards Mecca, as enjoined by the Koran. The *qibla* wall usually contains a number of *mihrabs* or arched recesses; these provide more of a focus than a wall can, and also, because of their pointed shape, indicate more emphatically the direction of prayer. The space in front

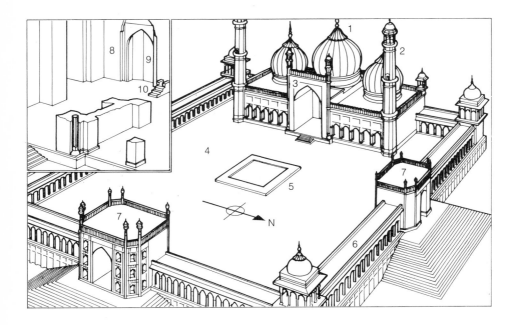

Parts of an Indian
mosque
1. sanctuary (*liwan*);
2. minaret; 3. *iwan*;
4. courtyard (*sahn*);
5. tank (*hauz*);
6. cloister (*riwaq*);
7. gateways.
Inset: section of the
sanctuary, showing 8.
qibla wall; 9. *mihrab*;
10. *minbar*.

of the wall is usually covered to form a prayer hall or sanctuary (*liwan*). When the congregation is particularly large — as on festival days or during the Friday prayer — the courtyard (*sahn*) is used as an extension to the *liwan*. The *mihrabs* within are of course invisible to worshippers in the courtyard, but the arches of the screen — and especially the high central arch — serve to amplify their message in this further space.

Other standard features of a mosque include the *minbar* — the pulpit consisting of a short flight of steps situated to the right of the central *mihrab*, from which the Friday prayer is read; and the *hauz* or water tank, placed in the centre of the courtyard to enable the faithful to wash before prayer (again as enjoined by the Koran). The courtyard is often bordered by a cloister (*riwaq*) intended primarily to provide shade, though sometimes used to house a *madrasa* (religious school).

Within the old city of Shahjahanabad there are two other major mosques of the Mughal period. The **Fatehpuri Masjid**, built by one of the emperor's wives in 1650, stands at the western end of Chandni Chowk. This location is in some ways superior to that occupied by the Jami Masjid, but it lacks the advantage of high ground. The design is simpler than that of the Jami Masjid, with a screen of only seven arches surmounted by a single dome, but these fewer parts are less well composed, and the general effect is somewhat gauche. A more successful imitation is the **Zinat-ul-Masjid**, situated in the Daryaganj district ((near the old Faiz Bazar). This is a much smaller mosque but it retains the relative proportions of the Jami Masjid, and so recaptures its elegance and balance. Built in 1710 by a daughter of Aurangzeb, it is mostly free of the florid detailing typical of such late Mughal work; though the bold decoration on the domes replaces the delicate pin-stripe of the Jami Masjid's domes with pyjama stripes.

The palace of Shah Jahan's new city lies on its eastern edge, where its two main thoroughfares meet. This site was chosen in 1638, a foundation stone was laid in the following year, and the palace was ready for occupation by 1648. According to some contemporary records, it cost ten million rupees, of which half was spent on the palace apartments themselves, and half on the vast fortification wall within which they stand. It is the wall, built of red sandstone, which gives the whole complex its name Lal Qila, or Red Fort. The eight-sided wall is 2.5 km (1½ miles) in length and varies in height from 18–33m (60–110 ft). The long, straight side on the east was built along the bank of the Jumna (though the river has since changed its course and flows further away); the various short sides to the north and south, and the long western side, are all surrounded by a moat (now dry) originally connected to the river. By the wall's north-east corner is a smaller and older fort, Salimgarh, which was built by Islam Shah Sur in 1546, as a defence against the return of the deposed Humayun; Jahangir added a bridge to this small fort, which Shah Jahan's wall abuts.

The wall is of a simple and grand design, with its smoothly dressed surface articulated by heavy string-courses and a fringe of merlons. It is pierced by two major gates which are aligned with the city's two arterial streets and so link the palace firmly to its setting. The gates are named — as was customary — after the cities towards which they face: the Lahore Gate is on the western side and the Delhi Gate on the south (facing the site of the older capitals).

The Red Fort, Delhi (from a plan made before the additions and destruction of the mid-19th century; not to scale)
1. Lahore Gate;
2. Chatta Chowk;
3. Delhi Gate;
4. Naqqar Khana;
5. Diwan-i-Am;
6. Asad Burj;
7. Mumtaz Mahal;
8. Rang Mahal;
9. Khas Mahal;
10. Mussaman Burj;
11. Diwan-i-Khas;
12. Hammam;
13. Moti Masjid;
14. Sawan Mahal;
15. Hayat Bakhsh Bagh; 16. Bhadon Mahal; 17. Nahr-i-Behisht; 18. Shah Burj; 19. Mehtab Bagh.

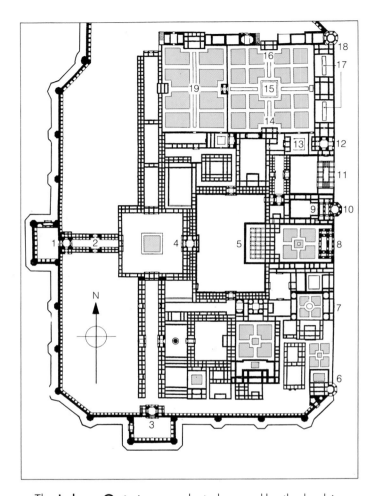

The **Lahore Gate** is somewhat obscured by the barbican added in front of it by Aurangzeb. Once all of its defences have been negotiated, it channels the visitor into a long, covered passage known as **Chatta Chowk**. The passage is lined with stalls designed to house a market, for the use of the inhabitants of the palace (so the tourist shops now occupying the stalls provide, at least, an authentic atmosphere). Chatta Chowk leads into a large space which once formed a crossroads, as at this point a broad street ran across the fort from north to south, ending at the Delhi Gate. This street divided the purely military zone of the fort, to its west, from the palace, to its east. Today, the army occupies an area in the northern part of the fort, and the dividing street together with the square where it passed the end of the Chatta Chowk, have disappeared.

All that remains of the square is a large red sandstone pavilion on its far side, opposite the market; this is the entrance gate of the palace, known as the Naubat or **Naqqar Khana** after the drum house contained in its upper storey (a standard feature at the entrances of Indian palaces). Music was played from it five times a day, and more on festive days. It is sometimes also known as the Hathiyan Pol (Elephant Gate) as it marks the point where visitors were required to dismount from their elephants. (The lost statues of elephants — from which the alternative name is often wrongly supposed to derive — were sited not here but outside the Delhi Gate.) The fullest description of this palace in use is that given by François Bernier, who visited it in 1663, early in the reign of Aurangzeb (when its creator was still alive, but imprisoned by his son, in Agra). The music issuing from the Naqqar Khana particularly intrigued Bernier:

> To the ears of an European recently arrived, this music sounds very strangely, for there are ten or twelve hautboys, and as many cymbals, which play together ... On my first arrival it stunned me so as to be insupportable: but such is the power of habit that this same noise is now heard by me with pleasure; in the night, particularly, when in bed and afar, on my terrace this music sounds in my ears as solemn, grand, and melodious.

The musicians' gallery now houses a small museum, so that its once open arches are closed by wooden screens which

The Lahore Gate of the Red Fort.

57

destroy much of the depth and variety of the façades. But there is still a grandeur in the outline of the building, and a delicacy in its relief ornament. It gives access to another large space beyond: now an open lawn, this was originally bordered by arcades and served as the courtyard of the huge pavilion at its eastern end.

This pavilion is the **Diwan-i-Am** (Hall of Public Audience) where the emperor heard petitions from members of the public, chiefly on judicial matters. It was also used for the reception of some important visitors, and the conducting of certain affairs of state. It is a hypostyle hall of red sandstone, nine bays wide and three deep. The twelve-sided columns support foliated or cusped arches. This type of arch is typical of Shah Jahan's architecture: the shape has its origins in early Indian prototypes (both Buddhist and Hindu); it had been further developed in the Muslim architecture of Bengal, and had more recently been re-adopted in Rajput architecture; but in Shah Jahan's buildings it was brought to the splendid maturity exemplified here. The arches and columns were originally plastered and decorated with paint and gilding, and rich draperies hung between them, so that the whole effect was more one of opulence than of the present solemn splendour.

Against the centre of the far wall of the hall, stands the emperor's throne balcony. Built of white marble, its base is carved in relief and its ornate canopy is decorated with *pietra dura* work. In front of the throne is a low bench — the seat of a minister, who acted as an intermediary between the emperor and his petitioner. On the wall behind the throne there is more *pietra dura* work; this includes a number of small panels depicting birds and flowers which are Italian in style. These panels were for a long time supposed to have been executed or inspired by Italian craftsmen employed by Shah Jahan; they therefore gave rise to a theory that Indian craftsmen learned the technique of *pietra dura* from Italians, and that the profusion of such decoration in Shah Jahan's many buildings marks a profound European influence. This theory was wishful thinking by Europeans, eager to claim a stake in such fine work. The technique developed quite separately in India and is usually characterised by a quite distinct style. The Italian-style panels here are in fact authentic Italian pieces, which were imported ready-made; their locally made background includes some Indian imita-

The throne of the Diwan-i-Am in the Red Fort.

tion of their bird figures, but is otherwise typically Mughal in style.

From François Bernier's account, we can gain an impression of this throne balcony and the hall in use:

> The Monarch every day, about noon, sits upon his throne, with some of his sons at his right and left; while eunuchs standing about the royal person flap away the flies with peacock's tails, agitate the air with large fans, or wait with undivided attention and profound humility to perform the different services allotted to each. Immediately under the throne is an enclosure, surrounded by silver rails, in which are assembled the whole body of Omrahs [nobility], the Rajas, and the Ambassadors, all standing, their eyes bent downwards, and their hands crossed. At a greater distance from the throne are the Mansebdars or inferior Omrahs, also standing in the same posture of profound reverence. The remainder of the spacious room, and indeed the whole courtyard, is filled with persons of all ranks, high and low, rich and poor.

As Bernier's description suggests, the Diwan-i-Am was used partly as a place of public display, where a wide cross-section of the emperor's subjects could gain some degree of access to him, and observe his magnificence. This accounts for its location on the outer edge of the main palace area. There are enough architectural elements in front of it — the Lahore Gate, the Naqqar Khana and the hall's deep courtyard — to ensure that any visitor is properly intimidated before he reaches it; but still it lies on the perimeter of the part of the palace where the emperor lived. All the private apartments lie behind.

The private palace consists of a line of separate pavilions along the eastern edge of the fort. From their common raised terrace, level with the top of the fort wall, they afford a view of the river plain and catch an unobstructed breeze. They are linked together by a water channel which runs in a straight line down the whole length of the terrace, passing through the core of each pavilion; this is known as the Nahr-i-Behisht, the Stream of Paradise.

The most southerly two of the surviving five pavilions of the row, were part of the *zenana*, or women's quarters (always distinct in a Mughal palace from the men's quarters, the *mardana*). The **Mumtaz Mahal**, at the far end, has been converted into a museum. A little to its north is the larger and finer **Rang Mahal** (a third *zenana* pavilion which stood

A Mughal woman in
a palace apartment.

between them has disappeared). The Rang Mahal was the
main resort for the women, and a lavish one. Cusped arches
supported on broad piers divide the internal space into
connecting apartments. The original ceiling, according to a
contemporary author, was 'gilded and ornamented with
golden flowers'; some parts still retain their mirror-work
decoration, and the walls have marble relief carving. In the
centre of the hall, the Nahr-i-Behisht runs into a marble

basin, whose sculpted floral forms were designed to agitate the flowing water. In front of the Rang Mahal lay a formal garden (the ruins of which remain) surrounded by other *zenana* ranges (now quite gone).

The next pavilion to the north is the **Khas Mahal**, containing the private chambers of the emperor. Though comparatively small, this pavilion consists of four distinct parts. On its southern side (facing the Rang Mahal) is a veranda, sometimes called the Baithak (sitting room); its ceiling is exquisitely painted with a floral geometrical design in gold and white, with touches of blue and green. In the centre of the pavilion is a suite of three rooms which served as the *khwabgah* (bedroom). Protruding from the *khwabgah*, on the eastern side, is the Mussaman Burj — an octagonal tower built against the fort wall and surmounted by a breezy gazebo. From here the emperor performed the important daily ceremony of showing himself to the people to demonstrate that he was still alive. The gazebo served also as an imperial grandstand, as it overlooks the once narrow space between the base of the fort wall and the river, a space used for the staging of animal fights. On the northern side of the Khas Mahal is another suite of three rooms, called the Tasbih Khana (place for telling beads) where the emperor engaged in private prayer. Separating

The Baithak of the Khas Mahal in the Red Fort.

The Diwan-i-Khas in the Red Fort.

the central, somewhat open part of this suite from the corresponding part of the *khwabgah* is a perforated screen of extraordinary delicacy. Below it runs the all-connecting water channel; above it is a panel of relief carving which includes a depiction of the scales of justice, meant to indicate that Mughal rule was not only mighty but just.

The next, and the finest, of the pavilions is the **Diwan-i-Khas**, the Hall of Private Audience, where the emperor conferred with his ministers and was attended by his nobles. As in the Rang Mahal, cusped arches on heavy piers divide the space, creating a central hall with flanking aisles. The dados of the piers are ornamented with *pietra dura* depictions of flowers, using semi-precious stones; the tops of the piers and the arches are decorated with paint and gilding. The original ceiling was of silver, inlaid with gold (it has been replaced by a painted wooden one). On the north and south walls, below the cornice, is repeatedly inscribed a couplet attributed to Amir Khusrau:

Pietra dura decoration on a dado in the Diwan-i-Khas.

Agar Firdaus bar rue Zamin-ast/Hamin asto Hamin asto Hamin ast
['If there be a paradise on earth, it is here, it is here, it is here.']

This claim is not simply an Oriental hyperbole; in many respects the palace is conceived as an imitation of the paradise described in the Koran. With its Stream of Paradise and its formal gardens, it marks an attempt to build the Islamic paradise on earth. An inscription in the Khas Mahal suggests that the inhabitants of the celestial paradise might envy the emperor his finer dwelling, and the theme is repeated in other inscriptions with no sense of modesty or fear of sacrilege.

In some early accounts of the palace, the Diwan-i-Khas is called the *ghasl khana*, a name which literally means 'washing room'. This alternative term may have arisen from the location of the hall close to the baths, for these (usually called *hammam*) are contained in the next pavilion to the north, the fifth and last in the row. The *hammam* includes a series of bath chambers of the Turkish type, though with typical Mughal ornamentation: the pavements, pools and dados are lined with marble and inlaid with coloured stones.

The Diwan-i-Khas and the other pavilions of the range are

The interior of the Diwan-i-Khas.

(*Opposite*) The Moti
Masjid in the Red Fort.

among the buildings which exemplify the Mughal style at the peak of its development, and they are typical of the architecture of Shah Jahan. In certain aspects of its design, the palace follows traditional Islamic patterns. The planning and the massing of the palace, for example, are based on Islamic prototypes outside India: the single-storeyed, detached pavilions are grouped formally on a piece of level ground (which emphasizes the horizontality of the composition). On the other hand, the vocabulary of architectural forms still includes those motifs of Hindu origin which had long been used in Muslim buildings in India: most obvious are the *chattris* surmounting each pavilion at the corners of the roof, and the *chajjas* which shade the upper parts of the façades. But the Shah Jahani style is not simply an extempore mixture of ideas torn from disparate sources; the various elements have been modulated to form a new style, with its own logic and conventions. The complicated arrangement of small chambers within the Khas Mahal, for example, shows that even some of the planning principles were drawn from local traditions; while the *chattris* have been Islamicized by onion domes. Ideas from the two widely differing traditions are here not just assembled, but synthesized. This synthesis is given a particular emphasis by the type of arch used most commonly in all of the pavilions: not the Islamic pointed arch, nor the Hindu corbelled one, but the cusped arch — a form which had been developed over time by both traditions within India.

The stylistic unity is emphasized also by the uniform whiteness of the pavilions, achieved mostly by the use of marble facing. The extensive use of marble, and of high quality materials in general, is another of the hallmarks of Shah Jahani architecture, as too is the refinement and the opulence of the applied decoration.

To the west of the *hammam*, out of line with the other pavilions, is the tiny **Moti Masjid** (or Pearl Mosque). As its position suggests, this was an afterthought, added in 1659 by Aurangzeb, as a place for the emperor's private prayer. Its exterior presents only a solid and rather plain red wall; inside, everything is richly modelled in white marble. The prayer hall, raised above the level of the courtyard, is closed by a screen of just three arches. Some of the decorative carving — such as the capitals of the piers — sustains the peak of quality achieved during the previous reign. But there

64

The doorway of the
Moti Masjid.

are also already some indications of the decline which set in during Aurangzeb's reign. The domes over the eastern door are not full-bodied but carved in relief, so that what were once architectural forms are here turned into surface ornament: the architecture has become a picture of itself. And much of the detailing has become florid: the contours of the domes over the prayer hall are cluttered by a profusion of pinnacles, and the finials are grotesquely large in proportion. The former discreet horizontal emphasis has been replaced by more dramatic gestures, and the elegance by extravagance.

A large area to the north of the Moti Masjid is laid out as a formal garden, the **Hayat Bakhsh Bagh** (or Life-bestowing Garden). Its form follows the Persian paradise tradition, as introduced into India by Babur, for the square garden is divided into four parts by two bisecting water channels which meet in a central tank. The channel which runs on the north-south axis is also linked to a pavilion at either end. The names of these pavilions — Sawan and Bhadon — refer to the months of the monsoon, and so add to the garden's Persian character an element of an indigenous tradition, based on the celebration of monsoon rain. It is therefore especially appropriate that, when the water flowed, it appeared to have its source in them: each stands on a podium, at the top of which is a chute from which the water fell into the channel. The cascade passed over a set of niches in the front of the podium, designed to create some particularly beautiful effects, as a contemporary commentator recorded:

> In the niches, flower vases of gold and silver, full of golden flowers, are placed during the day-time, and at night, white wax candles which appear like the stars in the thin clouds, are lighted and placed inside the veil of water.

A third pavilion, of red sandstone, stands within the central tank. Added by the last emperor, Bahadur Shah Zafar, in 1842, it is known after him as the **Zafar Mahal**. It somewhat blocks the original axial vistas of the garden; and it is weak in design, with thin and flattened forms. But its island setting is a striking caprice, and continues the reference to local traditions by recalling the Rajput *jal mahals* or water palaces.

The Nahr-i-Behisht which links the main pavilions of the

palace, runs along the eastern edge of this garden. The water was drawn from the Jumna, through a tower (the **Shah Burj**) at the north-eastern corner of the fort, from where it began its straight course southwards. At the head of the channel within the garden, Aurangzeb added another pavilion, the **Burj-i-Shamali**. This contains a *chadar*, a marble chute, sculpted in such a way as to make the water spurt as it ran down, as well as to be an attractive design in itself. Further south, also on the bank to the east of the garden, is the tiny pavilion called the **Hira Mahal**, added by Bahadur Shah Zafar.

The *chadar* in the Burj-i-Shamali.

Compared with its counterpart in Agra, the palace in the Red Fort of Delhi is a unified whole. Its main parts were conceived all at once, rather than built up piecemeal over time, and though it has some later additions these have not destroyed the original basic pattern. However, it is much less well preserved than the Agra palace, for various historical reasons. The Agra palace certainly suffered at the hands of later occupiers and booty hunters, but Delhi bore the brunt.

The palace suffered greatly in the 18th century from marauders such as Nadir Shah, who sacked Delhi in 1739, and the Marathas, who stripped the silver ceiling from the Diwan-i-Khas. And the decline in imperial power brought a decline in the life-style of the palace's occupants: the Englishwoman Fanny Parks visited it in 1838 and found the Rang Mahal inhabited by a number of hags living in ghastly squalor, with the water in the ornamental pool black from their kitchen drains. It suffered again after the sepoy mutiny of 1857. When the last emperor became the figurehead of the mutiny, the Fort became its headquarters, and when in time it came into British hands, a great deal of destruction was done. The arcaded courts in front of the Diwan-i-Am and the Diwan-i-Khas were swept away; the Rang Mahal was put to use as a mess room, and the *zenana* apartments to the west of it were destroyed. Another garden, to the west of the Hayat Bakhsh, was covered by a barracks. All of this was declared essential on the grounds of military strategy, but the careless disregard for the palace's architectural merits contained too an element of reprisal.

After half a century of destruction and neglect, a programme of restoration of the surviving parts was begun by the Archaeological Survey in 1903. Though sometimes a little slowly, this programme is still continuing.

SAFDAR JANG'S
TOMB

In 1739, the nobleman Abul Mansur Khan, known by the title Safdar Jang, succeeded his father-in-law as Nawab (or governor) of the district of Oudh, in the northern part of the empire. Later, during the reign of the late Mughal emperor, Ahmad Shah (r. 1748–54), Safdar Jang became also the Wazir, or prime minister of the empire. He tended to act, however, without reference to his master, who therefore sought to remove him from this office, in 1753. Such was the decline in imperial authority at this period, that in order to achieve his dismissal, the emperor had to enlist the services of an ambitious young relation of the Nizam of Hyderabad, and engage in a costly war. (Success did the emperor no lasting good, since his young ally from Hyderabad subsequently deposed him too.)

Safdar Jang's tomb was built at the instigation of his son, in 1753–4. It stands at the opposite end of the long and straight Lodi Road from Humayun's tomb, and at the opposite end, too, of the development of the Mughal style. Humayun's tomb is one of the style's earliest distinctive

Safdar Jang's tomb.

statements, at once confident and yet experimental. Safdar Jang's tomb shares the same basic plan and form, and is recognizably a part of the same tradition; but it is the style's last major statement, at once retrospective and yet curiously irresolute. The severe pointed arches of Humayun's tomb are here replaced by cusped arches — and not the deep, sculptural ones found in Shah Jahani architecture, but shallow, frilly ones. The arches' more numerous foils are embellished by leaves carved in relief, which disrupt their rhythmic lines. The dome bulges from its narrow neck, an elegant but effeminate form, with none of the noble simplicity of the dome of Humayun's tomb. These changes are typical of the stylistic tendency of 18th-century India: towards flatter forms which are swamped by details, and towards elegance at the expense of vigour.

Detail of the Jami Masjid, Lucknow (*c*. 1840).

Though his career at the centre of imperial affairs ended with his overthrow, Safdar Jang had secured control of the district of Oudh for a family dynasty. His successors, beginning with his son Shuja-ud-daulah (r. 1753–75), continued to style themselves 'Nawab' and so nominally acknowledged the authority of the emperor, but in practice they became increasingly autonomous. By the end of the 18th century, Oudh had surpassed Delhi as the major seat of Islamic power in northern India. And its capital, Lucknow, became the major centre of new Islamic architecture, for what that was then worth: buildings such as the Bara Imambara and the Rumi Darwaza, built by Nawab Asaf-ud-daulah (r. 1775–97), and the later Jami Masjid (*c*. 1840), continue further the debasement of the Mughal style, prefigured in the tomb of the Nawabs' ancestor in Delhi.

AGRA
THE MUGHAL SHOW-CASE

The city of Agra, like Delhi, stands on the bank of the Jumna, but over a hundred and sixty kilometres (100 miles) downstream, in a position slightly more central in the Mughal domains. The city has an ancient Hindu origin, but it had been re-founded in 1505 by the pre-Mughal Sultan of Delhi,

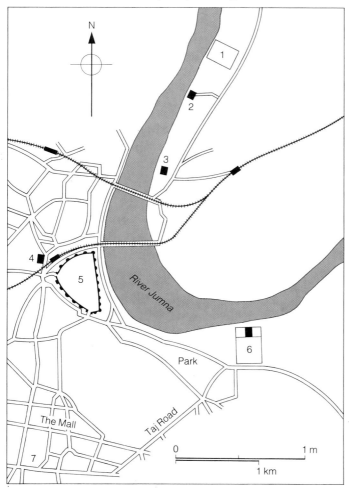

(*Opposite*) The gateway to Akbar's tomb, Sikandra.

Agra
1. Rambagh; 2. Chini ka Rauza; 3. Itimad-ud-daulah's tomb;
4. Jami Masjid;
5. Fort; 6. Taj Mahal;
7. cantonment area.

Sikander Lodi. In 1565, Akbar knocked down the small fort which Sikander had built by the river, and began to reconstruct it on a larger plan with stronger walls. Known at this point as Akbarabad, the city became the imperial capital, and it continued as such intermittently until Shah Jahan's move to Delhi in 1648. Almost nothing of the old city of Agra survives, and nearly half of the present city is a cantonment district built during the period of British rule. However, a number of its major Mughal monuments do survive, as isolated gems whose setting has gone. In the quality of these gems — in spite of the shorter span of its role as the capital — Agra surpasses even Delhi.

AGRA FORT

Akbar's fort in Agra shares a number of striking features with that built later by Shah Jahan in Delhi, and was evidently its model. The Agra fort walls are built of the same dressed red sandstone, and are surmounted by pointed merlons. Their size, too, is similar: they are 21 m (70 ft) high, and their combined length is 2.5 km (1½ miles). They define a less regular shape, but like its successor the Agra fort has one long and tolerably straight side to the east, on the river bank, near which the palace apartments are sited. The other sides together describe a bow, bulging to the west and protected by a moat. The main entrance (as in the Delhi fort) stands on the central axis on this western side; here there are two gates: the outer Delhi Gate, and close by an inner gate called the Hathi Pol.

The whole of the western side of the fort, however, is now closed to visitors, who must use instead the southern entrance, the **Amar Singh Gate**. This, too, is in parts. There is a simple gate at the end of the drawbridge, a loftier one within and at right angles to the first, and then a third and main part, again at right angles to the path. This awkward approach was designed to confuse any attacking force, and to ensure that there was too little space in front of each part for the effective use of battering devices. The inner part of the gate is a beautiful composition: a proportionally small central arch is flanked by massive buttresses, which are capped by domes and have an open gallery running across their tops and between them. This design is an imitation of the entrance gate added to the Rajput fort of Gwalior by Raja Man Singh Tomar around 1500. The use of brilliant blue

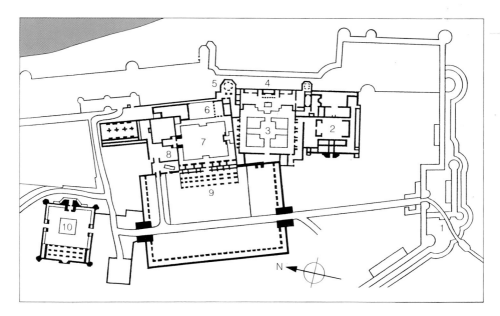

The palaces in Agra Fort
1. Amar Singh Gate;
2. Jahangiri Mahal;
3. Anguri Bagh;
4. Khas Mahal;
5. Mussaman Burj;
6. Diwan-i-Khas;
7. Macchi Bhawan;
8. Nagina Masjid;
9. Diwan-i-Am;
10. Moti Masjid.

tile decoration enhances the similarity, although the geometric patterns used here are purely Islamic.

Immediately beyond the Amar Singh Gate is a long straight ramp leading up to the palaces, and bordered by sheer walls. This again is a defensive measure: any force moving up the ramp (the only means of ingress) would be an easy target to defenders stationed on the top of the walls. The very name of the Amar Singh Gate is a further reminder of the violence which often disrupted the elegance of Mughal court life, for it is named after a Rajput nobleman who had created a disturbance in the palace and was cut down here while attempting to escape.

Straight in front of the top of the ramp is a gateway into the courtyard of the Diwan-i-Am, the Hall of Public Audience, which is situated (like its counterpart in Delhi) at a point where it can be visited without violation of the privacy of the rest of the palace. But the Diwan-i-Am belongs to a later phase of the palace's development: it is one of the embellishments made by Shah Jahan before his move to Delhi. If, instead of entering the Diwan-i-Am court, the visitor turns first to the right (or east), he will face an older structure — the long and imposing front of the **Jahangiri Mahal**. This was built by Akbar in about 1570, and it is the only major palace apartment within the fort which survives from his reign. Some authorities suppose from its name that it served as the residence of Akbar's heir, Jahangir; but this is a shaky inference, since Jahangir adopted that title only after his accession. And from the lack of openings in the main front and from the internal arrangements, it is clear that the building was a *zenana* (or women's palace).

In the centre of its main front is a large *iwan*, over which are panels of geometrical mosaic-work. Across the rest of the façade marches a blind arcade of pointed arches, picked out with white marble inlay. Each of these arches has a fringe of tassels on its intrados — a decoration copied from the 14th-century monuments of the Khilji and Tughluq Sultans of Delhi. These Islamic motifs are complemented by some of Hindu derivation, including the *jarokhas* (or balconies) protruding from the central section, the *chajja* running across the top of the façade, and the domed *chattris* which frame its ends. In terms of cultural mixture, the formula seen here is typical of a great deal of Indo-Islamic architecture of the period up to and including the early years of Akbar's reign: an essentially Islamic scheme is modified by the insertion of a few Hindu forms.

The interior of the Jahangiri Mahal, however, presents a very different appearance. In the ranges surrounding its central courtyard, the few Islamic features are overwhelmed by a profusion of ornately carved Hindu brackets and columns. The arches of the main openings are not pointed but made up of carved corbels, and other doorways are square-headed. The *chajja* is supported on fabulously rich and complicated brackets, and the upper storey is positively choked with them. The courtyard is flanked, to north and south, by large halls; the ceiling of the northern one is supported on giant stone beams decorated with fantastic animals. The whole conception of this courtyard and its halls is taken (like that of the Amar Singh Gate) from the palace of Man Singh Tomar in the fort of Gwalior. This degree of Hindu influence might seem less surprising when it is remembered that the Mughal emperors frequently employed local craftsmen on their architectural projects. It is probable that many of those responsible for the Jahangiri Mahal were Hindus, trained in local traditions. The preponderance of Hindu forms is an indication of the broadmindedness and liberalism of the patron, who employed craftsmen

The inner courtyard of the Jahangiri Mahal, Agra Fort.

of a different religion and cultural background to himself, and allowed them to implement their own ideas. As so often in Indian art history, design ideas have crossed a denominational boundary, not because they have been copied, but because the craftsmen who best practised them crossed that boundary.

The appearance of a few pointed arch windows on the upper storey, and of some geometric patterns in the relief carving on the piers, suggests that the craftsmen had some Muslim overseers or collaborators who broadened their repertoire. But in spite of these few Islamic touches, the design of the courtyard is essentially Hindu. It therefore presents a significant contrast with most earlier Indo-Islamic buildings, in which the balance of contribution is the other way round: usually until this point, it was a basically Islamic scheme which was modified by Hindu touches. This is true even of the buildings from the early years of Akbar's reign, such as Humayun's tomb, the Afsarwala mosque and tomb, Ataga Khan's tomb, and the Khairul Manazil Masjid — all built in Delhi in the 1560s. The walls of the Agra fort, and even the external façade of the Jahangiri Mahal itself also follow the long-established formula. The design of the inner courtyard disregards all these precedents. The change which it registers is much more than a shift in emphasis between the two contributing traditions; it marks the adoption of a more fundamental kind of Hinduization.

This new approach was employed in a number of other projects in the middle years of Akbar's reign. They include, most famously, the palace complex built at Fatehpur Sikri between 1571 and 1585 (which is discussed in the next chapter). They also include the palace apartments which were built by Akbar in the fort of Allahabad from 1583 onwards. These apartments are now substantially destroyed and are not accessible to visitors, but one of them was arguably the finest columned hall ever built in the Hindu style (see p. 137).

In these palaces, as in the Jahangiri Mahal at Agra, Islamic forms were not completely banished: a few Islamic openings or passages of decoration are also included. This has led many writers to describe the Akbari style of the 1570s and '80s as a 'synthesis' or 'fusion' of India's two main architectural traditions. Some writers depict the style as a reflection of the spirit of co-operation inherent in Akbar's

A courtyard of the Man Mandir, the Rajput palace in Gwalior (c. 1500).

approach to government. Clearly, Akbar's encouragement of local design is logically consistent with some of his poltical policies, but it is hard to see how the style of his buildings could justly be called a synthesis. In a synthesis, components are changed through contact. In Akbari buildings we often find a mixture of various traditional forms and patterns, treatments of space and structural methods, which are drawn from different sources; but none of these components has been modified through contact. Each is merely redeployed in an unfamiliar context, juxtaposed with alien components but not changed in itself. The style is not a synthesis but a mixture. It is an exotic medley.

This distinction is not just semantic pedantry; it is a matter of perceiving artistic ideals. For (as was argued with regard to the Delhi palace) a proper fusion of the two traditions was successfully achieved later. In the architecture of Shah Jahan, disparate forms and ideas are not simply assembled, they are modified and fused to create something new. In Akbari buildings such as the Jahangiri Mahal, plainly something quite different was being attempted. From their design, it appears that in the 1570s the craftsmen were not even aiming at a cultural synthesis — that was not then an artistic ideal. They were aiming instead at collecting — perhaps even contrasting — various favourite things. On the upper storey around the central courtyard, pure Islamic pointed windows alternate with pure Hindu carved brackets. This wilfully bizarre juxtaposition does not suggest craftsmen attempting to evolve a new homogeneous style; it suggests craftsmen drawing on established traditions in a spirit of adventurous eclecticism.

Beyond the Jahangiri Mahal's central courtyard, is another, more open court, with a view of the river. Originally, to the north of this palace, there were other apartments built by Akbar, presumed to have been of the same red sandstone. But these were swept away by Shah Jahan, to make space for his own palaces of white marble, built in the early years of his reign, before the transfer of the capital to Delhi (that is between 1627 and 1648). Most of the rest of the palace complex as it survives is the work of Shah Jahan. The extravagance of his replacement of durable buildings is a measure of changing tastes, and also of the association which he made between architecture and political power — an association which was common throughout India at this period. Like the other Mughals, Shah Jahan was conscious and proud of his dynasty, but he sought to establish his individual importance within that context. By re-creating the physical environment of the court, he could more easily associate both it and its achievements with himself; it would have been harder to sustain the required dignity in an outdated and hand-me-down palace. Contemporary kings and dukes in Europe had, of course, a similar view: the remodelling of ancestral estates was common practice there too. The notion that an inherited architectural environment can actually enhance the dignity of the user through historical associations, is a comparatively modern view.

At the southern end of the range of Shah Jahan's palaces (and in the next major court to the north of the Jahangiri Mahal) is the **Anguri Bagh**, or Grape Garden. This is a formal garden of the *charbagh* type, with a marble tank in its centre. Its four beds are subdivided by low curbs in a pattern of complicated interlocking shapes (originally accentuated by the colours of the flowers). On the eastern side is a terrace with three pavilions — the serene **Khas Mahal** (built in 1636), flanked by small pavilions with copper roofs. The curved central sections of these roofs are of the *bangaldar* type — so called because the shape was based on the roof of the Bengali village hut. It was first adopted in a lithic version in the sultanate architecture of Bengal, and was later much used in Rajput architecture.

In the middle of the terrace is a pool with a foliated edge and fountains; the water ran from this pool, down a slope

The Anguri Bagh, Agra Fort.

decorated with delicately coloured chevrons, fell in a cascade in front of a set of niches in the face of the terrace, and so flowed into the garden. A retreat from these dazzling effects of water and marble in the sunlight, was offered by the pavilions' interiors. These were cooler and more shaded when their arcades were hung with *tattis* — screens made from grass and kept wet — which cooled and scented any breeze. Alternatively, and especially in the colder seasons, the arcades were hung with embroidered draperies. In the subdued light inside, the occupants could study the intricate and subtle surface decoration. When their taste for such finery was jaded, they could look out from the backs of the pavilions, over the fort wall, to the space between the fort and the river, where animal parades and fights were staged — an arrangement which was one of the many aspects of this palace complex later re-created in the fort at Delhi.

As the name of the Khas Mahal denotes, this was the main private palace of the emperor. The local legend which assigns each of the flanking pavilions to one of Shah Jahan's two daughters, gives a charming but inaccurate picture of Mughal court life. Such pavilions were not devised for any single individual or any specific function; each is an open and adaptable space, which could be used for a variety of purposes. The rooms of Indian palaces were furnished only by carpets, draperies and bolsters; they did not, like European rooms, contain large immovable items of furniture such as dining tables and beds, which by assisting one, preclude other activities. An Indian ruler was not obliged to move to another room if he chose to sleep after a meal, for example; all he had to do was instruct an attendant to rearrange the bolsters.

These three pavilions by the Anguri Bagh are typical of the Mughal style during the Shah Jahani period. That style is often described as essentially Persian in character, and is contrasted with the Indianized style of Akbari buildings such as the adjacent Jahangiri Mahal. It is true that the treatment of space — the geometrical planning of the pavilions and the formal layout of the garden — marks a return to a basically Islamic scheme. But the popular view will not survive a comparison between the details of Shah Jahan's buildings and those of their supposed Persian models. The cusped arch, so ubiquitous here, is not a Persian form. And these buildings still contain the usual range of Hindu motifs

— the temple columns, corbel capitals, brackets, *chajjas* and *chattris* — which had always formed part of the repertoire of Indo-Islamic architecture.

What can be said is that in Shah Jahan's buildings these Hindu motifs are treated in a new manner, which is less directly imitative of the Hindu antecedents. The temple columns and corbel capitals have been stripped of their rich carving and turned into simpler, smoother forms. The brackets supporting the *chajja* are similarly not replicas of those of an Indian temple, but derived from them. And as in the Delhi palace, the *chattris* have Islamic domes. Through these subtle changes, the indigenous motifs have lost their specifically Hindu identity; they therefore contrast less strongly with the Islamic components, and are bound with them into a new style. The unity is assisted by the use of the cusped arch and the *bangaldar* roof — forms which had, in various versions, been widely used in India in the past, and so also had no exclusive association.

In other words, that synthesis with which the builders of Akbari palaces such as the Jahangiri Mahal are often wrongly credited, was actually achieved here. Shah Jahan's palaces, no less than Akbar's, draw on India's two main traditions; but here the various parts are combined, not simply in a collage, but in a new and resolved style. It is that resolution which gives the buildings their appearance of purity. There is no longer an exuberant eclecticism suggesting delight at diversity, but instead a dignified unity suggesting confidence in a new order. The purity which some writers have supposed to be Persian is in fact Mughal, and in the pavilions of the Anguri Bagh it makes its debut: here Mughal architecture comes of age.

At the north-east corner of the Anguri Bagh is a suite of rooms called the **Sheesh Mahal**; the name literally means 'glass palace' and refers to the mirror-work decoration over its walls. Just outside the garden, at the same corner, is the **Mussaman Burj** (or 'octagonal tower'; the name is sometimes abbreviated to Saman Burj or corrupted to Jessamine Burj). Crowned by an octagonal copper dome, this gazebo stands (like its namesake in Delhi) on a bastion protruding from the fort wall, and affords magnificent views of the river. It is quite the loveliest apartment of the Agra palace, with exquisite marble reliefs on its dados, *pietra dura* on its columns and walls, a sculpted pool in the floor of its outer

The Mussaman Burj,
Agra Fort.

chamber, pierced screens over its doorways, and banks of niches which held lamps and scent bottles (in a manner more decorative than practical).

Like other Mughal decoration of its period, this work is startling in its refinement. As in the architecture itself, the inspiration is derived from varied sources. The geometrical patterns and stylized flowers are basically Islamic in conception, but there is an unusual fluidity in their treatment which suggests the hand of the Hindu draughtsman. In this sophisticated manner of blending, the contributing components have lost their individual identities and have become inseparable in something original and unique. Once again, it is a fusion which is the basis of the characteristically Mughal genius.

From the little court before the Mussaman Burj, steps lead up to the **Diwan-i-Khas** (the Hall of Private Audience). Completed in 1637, this is an open hall of a simpler form than other Mughal pavilions of such importance, since its internal space is not subdivided. The bordering arcade is particularly fine as it is supported not on the usual broad piers but on elegant, twelve-sided columns in pairs. The columns' flared bases are decorated with both coloured inlay and mono-chrome relief — a typically Mughal combination which works so unexpectedly well. The hall stands at one end of a broad terrace on which are also two thrones. To the east is an uninterrupted view of the river. On the other side, the terrace overlooks a large courtyard, originally the site of a garden, surrounded by ranges known as the **Macchi Bhawan** (or 'fish building'), from which name it is inferred that the garden once contained a tank.

Near the north-west corner of the upper gallery of the Macchi Bhawan is the tiny **Nagina Masjid**, a mosque reserved for the use of the women of the court. The fort contains two other mosques: the even smaller **Mina Masjid**, for the private use of the emperor, located near the Mussaman Burj; and the much larger **Moti Masjid**, or Pearl Mosque, to the north of the palaces. The latter has a screen of seven arches and a spacious courtyard. It was completed as late as the 1650s, showing that the architectural embel-lishment of the fort continued even after it had ceased to be the main imperial residence: it was still used occasionally, and was always maintained by a garrison. The Moti Masjid has been much admired by critics, though more for the purity

The Moti Masjid, Agra Fort.

of the white marble scheme than for any sculptural coherence: its three equal domes are rather small and fail to dominate the façade of the prayer hall satisfactorily. (At the time of writing, it has long been closed to visitors.)

From the western side of the Macchi Bhawan, steps lead down to the last major pavilion of the palace, the **Diwan-i-Am** (the Hall of Public Audience). This is a gigantic hypostyle hall. Three bays deep and nine bays long, it is of the same proportions as its counterpart in Delhi, but it is on a substantially larger scale. It is similarly built of red sandstone, but retains its plaster covering. In its back wall are screens through which the women could watch the proceedings unobserved; in the centre of the wall is a decorated recess screened by three trefoil arches.

In this recess, Shah Jahan spent much of his morning, while his nobles and courtiers stood in strict hierarchical order on the hall's floor. Much of the business which they conducted in the hall was of an executive kind, as any consultative process took place more privately in the Diwan-i-Khas. Here, there was more formal announcement and administration than discussion. While the work was going on, the tedium might be relieved by a parade of animals in the courtyard — the Mughal version of a military review, with elephants and horses. Occasionally the business of the day was hearing petitions from individuals, with the emperor acting as judge between parties in dispute. The declared purpose of these sessions was to give humble citizens access to their emperor. It has been suggested that this purpose could be undermined by the court officials, who acted as intermediaries and were probably able to control just who appeared and what was said. But even such limitations would not detract from the ceremonial and symbolic purposes of the sessions. They provided an opportunity for the emperor to appear in the role of Solomonic judge, and for his subjects to be dazzled by his splendour. For such theatrical activities, the Diwan-i-Am was a perfectly designed stage set.

For the hall's already ornate recess, Shah Jahan commissioned the famous Peacock Throne. Probably Shah Jahan's greatest enthusiasm was for gems, and as his official biographer explained:

In the course of years many valuable gems had come into the imperial jewel-house, each one of which might serve as an ear-

drop for Venus, or would adorn the girdle of the Sun. Upon the accession of the emperor, it occurred to his mind that, in the opinion of far-seeing men, the acquisition of such rare jewels and the keeping of such wonderful brilliants can only render one service, that of adorning the throne of empire.

The interior of the Diwan-i-Am, Agra Fort.

The emperor meant this quite literally: he instructed the superintendent of his goldsmith's department to build a throne which would incorporate his gem collection. The work took seven years and was completed in 1634. The throne was built on the usual Mughal pattern, with a cushioned cradle shaded by a canopy. But in this case, the canopy was covered in enamel work and studded with individual gems, its interior was thickly encrusted with rubies, garnets and diamonds, and it was supported on twelve emerald-covered columns. The design incorporated one ruby valued at a hundred thousand rupees, and two jewelled figures of peacocks. The throne was later transferred to the palace in Delhi, from where it was looted by Nadir Shah of Persia in 1739, and subsequently broken up.

This throne was devised, of course, as a means of display — but not only of imperial wealth. Just as the hall of the Diwan-i-Am served as a show-case for court ritual, so the jewelled throne served as a suitable setting for the display of the palace's most prized jewel — the emperor himself — as

Shah Jahan in Durbar.

an object of veneration before his subjects. This kind of display echoed the Hindu temple ritual of *darshan*, in which the image of the deity is revealed to the worshippers. The shape of Mughal thrones reinforced the connection, for they often took the form of a *jarokha*. The *jarokha's* architectural antecedent was a niche in the Hindu temple wall, which accommodated a religious sculpture (as in the temples of Khajuraho, for example). The niche was adapted as a window, and also as a throne balcony, in early Rajput palaces such as those at Chitor and Gwalior. From this source it was introduced into Mughal architecture, in both its secular uses. And these uses were combined with the custom of *darshan* in the daily ritual when the emperor showed himself to the public (to demonstrate that he was still alive) from a window balcony in the fort wall. In such ways the Mughals made use of Indian traditions to enhance their own grandeur, while at the same time (though inadvertently perhaps) revealing the extent to which they had become assimilated in the culture of the land they ruled.

Just outside the fort, on its north-western side, is the **Jami Masjid**, or principal mosque of the city. It was originally connected to the fort's Delhi gate by a courtyard; but since the period of British iconoclasm which followed the mutiny of 1857, it has been separated from it by an intrusive railway line. Completed in 1648, the mosque was built on the orders of Jahanara. She was the elder daughter of Shah Jahan, who attended the ageing emperor in his years of captivity, when Aurangzeb had usurped the imperial throne and imprisoned his father in Agra fort. Jahanara's filial fidelity still excites much popular admiration, especially as it contrasts with the attitude of her younger sister, Roshanara, who was sympathetic to the cause of their brother. The mosque is not one of the most successful of Mughal designs: the openings in the screen of the prayer hall are somewhat small and separated, so that the screen seems heavy and closed. But the jaunty zig-zag bands on the three domes lend an attractive and playful touch.

Some account of the personality and career of Akbar was given in the Introduction. The tomb of this greatest of the Mughal emperors lies at Sikandra, a district named after Sultan Sikander Lodi and situated 8 km (5 miles) outside the

AKBAR'S TOMB, SIKANDRA

city, to the north-west. Like that of his father in Delhi, Akbar's tomb stands in a large, square, walled garden, which is entered through a gateway in the southern side. This gateway is a stately composition; its high central arch is flanked by others on two storeys, and the surfaces around the arches are covered in geometric and arabesque designs in bold mosaic-work. On the roof are four white tapering minarets; these make the building somewhat resemble an upturned commode, but they add a delicate touch which tempers the austere shapes of the pointed arches.

The garden within is a standard *charbagh*, with a simpler arrangement of channels than in the garden of Humayun's tomb, in spite of its much greater size. The planting here is now a little erratic; originally (as in other such tomb gardens) there was a dense but regular planting of fruit trees and flowering shrubs. The garden is now the haunt of deer and rhesus monkeys.

In the centre is the tomb itself, one of the most curiously hybrid of Mughal creations. The massive podium, with its arcade of severe, four-centred arches, is 9 m (30 ft) high; and in the centre of each side, an *iwan* bordered by mosaic panels reaches to twice that height. Above this solid arcuate base, rises a pyramid of airy cages. The three central storeys, of red sandstone, are almost entirely trabeate in construction and appear from outside to have no solid parts. Perched on top of them is a courtyard surrounded by a white marble veranda; the openings here are again arched, and contain delicate *jalis* of various geometric designs. In the centre of the courtyard is a simple cenotaph; this one is, of course, purely symbolic — as in most Mughal tombs — the genuine sarcophagus is placed directly but far below its dummy, in a crypt underneath the building.

Some of the decorative details of this tomb are exquisite, and the building as a whole is not without charm and interest; but in the relation of its parts it is decidedly idiosyncratic. The disparity in style between the central storeys and the base suggests a change of mind by the craftsmen half-way through construction. There is a *prima facie* case for suspecting Akbar's son and successor, Jahangir, of being responsible for this lack of coherence. Like his father, Akbar had neglected to build his tomb in his lifetime. The work began in 1605, the year of Akbar's death, and it continued until 1612. Jahangir, according to his own

memoirs, visited the site in 1608 to inspect the work in progress, and was dismayed to find that 'it did not come up to my idea of what it ought to be'. He complained that the craftsmen had had the impertinence to build 'after a design of their own', and he set about explaining to the profession-als how these things were done, ordering changes to be made according to 'a settled plan'. Jahangir's account of this episode is too brief for us to be sure that it was the cause of the irresolute character of the tomb's design, but certainly the design shows every indication of having been devised by people with conflicting ideas about what it should be like.

Apart from its stylistic inconsistency (a quality which is, after all, not altogether unknown in buildings connected with Akbar) another curiosity of the design is the absence of a crowning feature, such as a dome. The building rises to a strangely flat top; the lines of the pyramid point to nothing. Some writers have believed that the builders intended to add a dome, basing their view on a statement to that effect by the English merchant William Finch, who visited the tomb when it was in construction. Certainly, a dome would improve the contours of the tomb, but it is hard to see how it would have been placed in relation to the topmost veranda.

Like other such complexes, the tomb and garden were conceived as an imitation of the Koranic heaven. Inscriptions on the gateway continue in words the reference to paradise

Akbar's tomb, Sikandra.

which is contained in the garden's very layout; and the place was sometimes called (for example by Jahangir) Behishtabad, or City of Heaven. Though the water channels, which are an essential part of this reference, are now dry, the garden retains its enchanting peacefulness. This quality was not created for the benefit only of the spirit of the departed: such gardens were intended for the enjoyment of the living. The 18th-century English artist and traveller William Hodges, was told that in former times the terraces of the tomb

> had coverings of gold cloth, supported by pillars of silver. Under the shade of these awnings the Mollahs or priests of the religion of Mahommed conversed with men of learning.

But the tranquillity has not been uninterrupted. The anti-Hindu policies of Akbar's great-grandson Aurangzeb, stirred much popular resentment, and especially vehement was the reaction of the Jat peasants of the Mathura district, just north of Agra. Having suffered the reimposition of the *jizya* (a tax on heathen worship) in 1679, and having witnessed the destruction of many temples including the great Kesava Deo temple in Mathura, the Jats broke out in rebellion. One of the expressions of their outrage was an assault on Akbar's tomb in 1691. They looted its bronze gates and much of its ornament, and according to one account, exhumed the body of the emperor to burn his bones. In view of Akbar's own policies of religious tolerance, this attack was an especially unfortunate act, but the grave of an ancestor was an easy target for the frustrated Jats, who were no historians.

ITIMAD-UD-DAULAH'S TOMB

On the far side of the Jumna from the Agra fort, one and a half kilometres (1 mile) upstream, stands one of the most beautiful of Mughal tombs. Though it is unpretentious in size, enormous energy and expense were lavished on its decoration, and it is important as a landmark in the development of the Mughal style. It contains the graves of a distinguished chief minister and his wife.

Mirza Ghiyas Beg was a Persian who, finding his fortunes failing at home, travelled to India. He and his wife reputedly suffered such hardship and bad luck on their journey that they considered abandoning their infant daughter. But the family succeeded in reaching their destination, where

Ghiyas Beg found employment at the court of Akbar. He rose in rank, and continued in service in Jahangir's reign, with the title Itimad-ud-daulah, or Pillar of the State. His daughter married a nobleman of Afghan descent, but he died while on service in Bengal, and the girl went as a young widow to live at court. There her beauty attracted the attention of Jahangir. Accordingly to a (probably fictitious) tradition, she repulsed his attentions at first; but in 1611 she agreed to marry him. Her name was Mehrunissa, but Jahangir called her Nur Mahal ('light of the palace') and later Nur Jahan ('light of the world'). Such was Jahangir's devotion to her, and such were her own abilities, that she became the most powerful woman in Mughal history, able to control state affairs from behind the *purdah* screen.

Nur Jahan did not work alone. Her powerful faction included her father, her brother Asaf Khan, and also for a while the young prince Shah Jahan. Nur Jahan initially favoured Shah Jahan for the succession; but when she saw the prince's precocious military prowess, she began to fear that by helping him to power she would be excluded from it herself, and she transferred her support to Shah Jahan's less remarkable brother, Shahriyar. She persuaded this step-son to marry her own daughter (from her first marriage). This move split the family faction, for her brother Asaf Khan had earlier married his daughter, Mumtaz Mahal, to Shah Jahan,

Itimad-ud-daulah's tomb.

89

Detail of one of the minarets.

whom he continued to support. In time, of course, it was indeed Shah Jahan who succeeded. But the family influence was not lost, for Shah Jahan's devotion to Mumtaz Mahal was as great as that of his father to her aunt.

The patriarch, Itimad-ud-daulah, died in 1622. According to Jahangir, he simply lost the will to live after the death of his wife. Jahangir also described the grief of Nur Jahan at the loss of her father, and it was she who commissioned the tomb which houses both her parents. It was completed in 1628.

The tomb stands, as usual, in a *charbagh*, entered in this case from the eastern side — a departure from the standard southward orientation, adopted probably to make use of the river as a backdrop to the composition. The shape of the tomb itself also marks a departure from precedent, and (with the exception of a later imitation of it) is unique. It is a low square building with an engaged minaret at each corner, and a square pavilion in the centre of the roof, capped by a low and angled dome. The overall shape is more intriguing than satisfying, seeming to indicate an experiment which was not fully resolved. The roof pavilion, for example, is overshadowed by the minarets and so does not act as a dominating focus, and it appears small in relation to the lower storey. The general form is suggestive less of a tomb than of a reliquary.

The impression of an enlarged precious object is enhanced by the surface decoration, which is the main glory

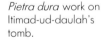

Pietra dura work on Itimad-ud-daulah's tomb.

of the building. The interior contains much stucco-work and painting, while the external surfaces are entirely covered with *pietra dura* in floral and geometrical designs. Though the patterns are rich, there is a certain restraint in the colour scheme of the inlay: it concentrates on black, grey and various shades of ochre. Together with the contemporary Chaunsath Khamba in Delhi, this tomb is the first example in Mughal architecture of a building faced entirely in white marble, and it provides the first example of a very extensive use of the *pietra dura* technique. Both features, and their combination, were to become common in the period following its construction.

A little to the north of Itimad-ud-daulah's tomb, and on the same side of the river, are two other monuments of interest from the Mughal period. The building now known as the **Chini ka Rauza** is believed to be the tomb of Afzal Khan, a Persian who served as a minister to Shah Jahan and died in 1639. It is now in a dilapidated state, but it retains some patches of the enamelled tile-work which once covered it. There is a Persian influence in the shape of the tomb: its severe geometric volumes have few openings and none of the usual Hindu embellishments. The tile-work, too, is Persian in both design and technique. It depicts stylized plants standing in niches, in a colour scheme which is basically blue and white, with touches of green, turquoise, yellow and orange. The patterns are composed with fragments of tile, embedded like mosaic pieces into the plaster which covers the brickwork. The tomb was the only building in India to have a complete covering of tiles of this kind. Its current name literally means 'China tomb' and refers to the tiles, in a manner which recognizes the role of Chinese influence in the development of such work in Persia.

A little further to the north is the **Rambagh**, a formal garden which was laid out by Babur and is one of the very few of his creations to survive. The garden was originally called Aram Bagh (or Garden of Rest) but the 'Aram' has been corrupted to 'Ram', after the Hindu god. The water channels are much narrower than those in other Mughal gardens; this is an indication of their early date, for such channels were originally intended more for irrigation than as a principal feature. The other architectural elements, however, are later additions, and parts of the garden plan have also been changed. It is believed that this garden was

Babur's temporary place of burial, before his body was moved to his tomb in Kabul.

THE TAJ MAHAL

The Taj Mahal.

All other Mughal architectural achievements, in spite of their splendours, are surpassed by the Taj Mahal — a work of such flawless beauty that one's initial astonishment at it never fades. It is the tomb of Arjumand Banu Begam, better known by her title Mumtaz Mahal (or Elect of the Palace) who married Shah Jahan in 1612. She was the granddaughter of Jahangir's chief minister, Itimad-ud-daulah, and also the

niece of that emperor's wife, Nur Jahan. As her aunt was stepmother to the prince, Shah Jahan, Mumtaz Mahal was his step-cousin. Though not his first, she became his favourite wife: one indication of his attentions is that in nineteen years of marriage she bore him fourteen children. In spite of this punishing timetable, she was expected to accompany her husband wherever his military career took him. It was while pregnant again and following him on campaign in the Deccan, that she died, in 1631, a few years after Shah Jahan's accession.

Her tomb takes its name from an abbreviation of her own. It was begun after her death, and took over twenty years to build, according to the French traveller Jean-Baptiste Tavernier who witnessed parts of the operation. Tavernier also noted that twenty thousand workmen were involved in the construction, and — a further indication of the energy and expense involved — that the scaffolding was of brick. *Firmans* (or edicts) issued by Shah Jahan to the Maharaja of Amber show that much of the marble and some of the masons who worked it were brought from Rajasthan; other materials and craftsmen are known to have come from other parts of India and even from neighbouring countries.

As in previous Mughal tombs, there is not one but a whole complex of buildings. The tomb itself stands on a podium with an elegant, tapering minaret at each corner. This ensemble stands on a terrace which it shares with two other buildings. To the west is a triple-domed mosque, while to the east is the mosque's *jawab* or echo. Oriented the wrong way, this third building could not be used for worship; it has been suggested that it was intended to accommodate visitors to the tomb, but evidently its primary function was simply to provide a balance to the mosque, and so preserve the symmetry of the composition. In front of the terrace is a giant *charbagh*, 300 m (1,000 ft) wide, with a marble pool in its centre. Together with the terrace, the garden is bordered by a high wall, which is punctuated by pavilions and gazebos, and pierced on the southern side by a stately gate.

Even this is not the end of the matter: outside the gate is an arcaded courtyard and, close by to the south and west, a number of other mosques and small tombs of sandstone and marble, pertaining to other wives of Shah Jahan. Each of these structures might have attracted some attention elsewhere, but here they are mere outbuildings.

The garden of the Taj
Mahal
1. tomb; 2. mosque;
3. *jawab*;
4. entrance gate.

The main jewel in all this setting, the Taj Majal itself, is at once original and yet familiar. Its perfection makes it unique, but certain aspects of its form and structure link it firmly to other examples of the Indo-Islamic tradition. Inside is a central octagonal hall, with four smaller octagonal halls grouped around it; these halls are contained within a basic plan which is almost square, but which has chamfered corners, making an irregular octagon. The internal grouping of halls is echoed on the roof, where a central dome is surrounded by those of four *chattris*. On each façade, arched recesses arranged in two storeys flank a high *iwan* in the middle; and the border around the *iwan* rises higher than the rest of the façade. All these patterns are reworkings of themes which had been adopted in earlier Islamic tombs in India. The most recent precedents are the tomb of Humayun (1560s) and that of Khan-i-Khanan (*c*. 1626), both in Delhi. But there are much earlier prototypes on which these models in turn were based. The use of an *iwan* in a raised, central section of the façade (or *pishtaq*) had been a common motif in India since the building of the tomb of Ghiyas-ud-din Tughluq in 1320. Octagonal planning and the clustering of domes are features of the tombs of the early 15th-century Sayyid sultans; and the arrangement of arched recesses in tiers on the exterior, is a common pattern in the tombs of the succeeding Lodi period.

Some writers have insisted that the design of the Taj Mahal is Persian — an analysis which ignores not only its more immediate derivation from those Muslim buildings within India mentioned above, but also, of course, the presence of certain Hindu elements, such as the *chajjas* below the lesser domes and the metal finials surmounting all the domes. The Indian roots of the Taj Majal are many, varied and deep.

A few parts of the design draw on the building's close neighbours. Minarets are unusual adjuncts to a tomb, but their use here is based on a couple of earlier experiments: their form is taken from those on the gateway of Akbar's tomb, while their position has been adapted from those of Itimad-ud-daulah's tomb. The Taj Mahal follows the latter building also in its materials — the white marble facing with *pietra dura* decoration — and in the use of the river as a backdrop to the architectural scheme. There is a departure from that model, though, and from other precedents, in the tomb's relation to its garden: in order to make the most of the landscape setting, the Taj Mahal stands not in the centre but at the margin of its garden.

In all the respects in which the Taj Mahal follows earlier Indo-Islamic tombs, it marks the apogee of a tradition, but it does not mark its end. There are later Mughal tombs which pursue the same themes and patterns further, though without repeating the success. One of these is the Bibi ka Maqbara in Aurangabad — a tomb built in 1678 for Rabia Daurani, a wife of Aurangzeb. The same basic form was used again nearly a century later, when the tomb of Safdar Jang was built in Delhi. These later examples are marred by florid detailing and by an etiolation of the architectural features.

The Taj Mahal is therefore a part of a sequence, from which it stands out only in quality, surpassing both its antecedents and its imitators. This superiority is achieved by a number of means. It is the result, most simply and crudely, of the building's great size. Each of its elevations measures 56 m (186 ft) across, some 9 m (30 ft) more than the elevations of Humayun's tomb; and its total height, including the top finial and the podium, is over 73 m (240 ft) — slightly higher than the Qutb Minar. Its success depends more importantly, though, on the proportions of its parts. To begin with, the height of the tomb without the finial and the podium is the same as each side of its plan, so that its extremities define a cube. And the corners of the building are chamfered at such a point as to make each angled face the same width as the

(*Above*) Detail of the Bibi ka Maqbara.

(*Right*) The Bibi ka Maqbara, Aurangabad.

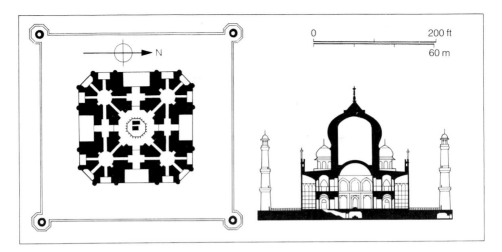

marginal parts of the main façades; thus between each *iwan* and the next are three equal sides which turn the corner smoothly and keep the eye for ever moving around the building's surfaces.

Finally, the peculiar success of the Taj Mahal depends on the delicacy of its decoration. Around the border of each *iwan* runs a Koranic inscription in a bold and rhythmic script. Most of the other decoration depicts flowers, a subject which refers to the paradise theme central to the conception of all such garden-tomb complexes. Some of the flowers are carved in relief on the marble dados of the building, inside and out. Others are inlaid in *pietra dura*; this work varies in scale from the huge motifs in the spandrels of the arches to the small chains on the borders of the dados, but the best work is on the cenotaphs themselves. These stand in the tomb's main chamber, with that of Mumtaz Mahal occupying the central position, and that of Shah Jahan — added after the deposed emperor's death in 1666 — standing asymmetrically to one side and distinguished as a man's tomb by the pen box carved on the top. As usual, the real sarcophagi lie in an underground chamber directly below. These are scarcely less ornate, but the dummy cenotaphs above are surrounded by an exquisite perforated screen, with *pietra dura* on its solid parts.

The *pietra dura* decoration employs a variety of coloured marbles and semi-precious stones, including cornelian, coral, jasper, onyx, amethyst, lapis lazuli, turquoise and

Plan and section of the Taj Mahal.

(*Above*) The screen and cenotaphs within the Taj Mahal.

(*Below*) Relief carving and *pietra dura* work on a dado of the Taj Mahal.

jade. The pieces are cut and matched with precision, and the craftsmen had a particular skill in using the gradations in a stone's surface to suggest the shade or colour variation on a flower's petal. There is therefore a certain tension in the designs between stylization and realism, and it is this tension which makes the work so sensitive and subtle. The contrast between the coloured designs and the monochrome relief carving works in a similar way. Scarcely less important than the intrinsic qualities of the decoration is the restraint with which it has been applied; it is often rich but it never chokes the architectural forms. The scale of the building helps in this respect, for the surfaces which are left plain are vast and bold.

As can happen with buildings of such distinction, the Taj Mahal has generated a number of myths. One of these relates to the asymmetrical placing of the cenotaphs: it is supposed that the inclusion of Shah Jahan's remains was a late improvisation, not originally intended. This supposition supports the story that Shah Jahan originally planned to build as his own tomb, a replica of the Taj Mahal in black marble, which would have stood opposite the original building on the far side of the Jumna, and be linked to it by a bridge. This theory has its origin in a statement by the French traveller Tavernier, who alleged that the plan was aborted because of Aurangzeb's usurpation of the throne. Many historians have been disposed to believe Tavernier's story, but this indicates a triumph of imagination over scholarship, for there is no corroborative evidence. And it has been pointed out that the asymmetrical arrangement of the cenotaphs has a precedent in Itimad-ud-daulah's tomb, where it was certainly not an improvisation.

An even more popular myth is that Europeans were involved in the Taj Mahal's design. Again, there is no credible foundation for the view, but it is worth examining for what it reveals about an episode in Western understanding of Indian architecture. Its basis is the contemporary statement by a Spanish Augustinian friar, Father Sebastian Manrique, that the Taj Mahal was designed by a Venetian jeweller named Geronimo Veroneo. Manrique did not know Veroneo; he was merely repeating a story he had heard. This evidence is of a sort which, taken alone, would not be seriously entertained by any dispassionate historian. For the many accounts by witnesses of the building's construction make no mention of European involvement. Descriptions by foreign travellers like Tavernier and Bernier do not discuss the designers at all, though in some cases it is clear that they assume them to be local. The official Mughal histories mention some of the designers by name. A couple of the names given suggest Persian or Turkish architects, but there is some disagreement between the various texts about the identity of the chief designer. This disagreement is perhaps an indication that no individual designer was paramount, and that — following standard Indian practice — several worked together. But in spite of this uncertainty, the Mughal texts do make clear that the architects were drawn from the Muslim world. And it is clear from the design of the building itself, which leans so heavily on local precedents, that at least some of the designers were from India.

Why, then, should Manrique's assertion ever have been believed? It was partly the result of a natural, if unscholarly, desire on the part of Westerners to claim a share in the masterpiece. Manrique offered them a fantasy which they wanted to believe in. But the idea appealed also to a less

innocent line of thought. Western attitudes to Indian architecture have varied over time and between individuals, and
throughout the time that the West has known India there
have been those who have sought sympathetically to
understand and explain Indian culture; but in the period
between the 1830s and the middle of the 20th century there
was also, especially among the British public, a certain strain
of contempt and dislike for it. For those who wanted to
believe that the Indian cultural tradition was worthless,
Manrique solved the puzzle of the Taj Mahal's undeniable
excellence, by attributing it to external contribution. The
argument was extended to include the *pietra dura* decoration common to many of Shah Jahan's buildings — this, too,
was believed to have been introduced by European
jewellers. These views were espoused in the early 20th
century by the otherwise reputable historian, Vincent Smith,
who argued the slender case most vociferously in his
determination to deprive India of the credit for creating the
Taj Mahal. Later scholars have rightly treated the theory with
scant regard.

In recent years, this myth informed by politics has given
way to another, informed by sentiment: the belief that the
principal designer was Shah Jahan himself. This is a charming but purely romantic idea. Shah Jahan was a great
patron, he was not an architect. Though patrons of architectural conceptions from palaces to kitchen extensions commonly believe that the design is mostly of their own making,
the truth is generally that it owes more to the trained
professionals whose ideas they select. There is no evidence
to suggest that Shah Jahan had anything more than this
usual patron's role.

The Taj Mahal has been represented in paintings and
photographs unnumbered times, but the original always
surpasses such depictions. It is bound to do so because of the
subtlety of the veined marble, and its manner of responding
to the changing light; these effects pictures cannot convey.
For this reason, too, the building is always a surprise,
however well prepared the visitor may be.

A further element of surprise is achieved by the grouping
of the satellite buildings. As one approaches the complex,
the tomb itself is concealed from view by the garden wall,
and it is only on walking through the southern gateway that
it is suddenly revealed, in a moment like the lifting of a bride's

veil. This is one aspect of an allegedly feminine quality which some (male) writers have, sometimes apologetically, identified in the building. Whether it is expressly feminine or not, the Taj Mahal certainly has a kind of sexual appeal, and this is due in no small part again to the main material, with its flesh-like surface. It is a seductive building; to dislike it requires a very determined cynicism which few can honestly sustain. It is a building so ethereal that when the setting sun or the moon shines on its dome, one may easily forget that it is a work of human labour; it seems to have been left here by people from another world. It transcends all the wildest fantasies about the East, for genies and magic carpets are mere banalities beside its sublime and incandescent loveliness.

The Taj Mahal seen across the River Jumna.

FATEHPUR SIKRI
THE MUGHAL ENIGMA

In the early years of his reign, Akbar was troubled by his lack of an heir; none among his large number of wives had succeeded in producing a son who survived beyond infancy. Akbar consulted in this matter a Muslim divine named Shaikh Salim. The shaikh was a member of the Chishti order, which Akbar already revered, and he lived the life of a recluse on a hill at Sikri, 40 km (25 miles) to the west of Agra. When the shaikh heard of the emperor's worries, he predicted the birth of three sons. Shortly after, a pregnant wife (a Rajput princess from Amber) was transferred to Sikri, along with some of her attendants, in order to live close to the shaikh and so enhance the auspiciousness of his prophesy. On 30 August 1569, she gave birth to a son. Later to be the emperor Jahangir, the child was at first named in honour of the shaikh, Salim. In March of the following year, another son was born, also to a wife who had lodged with the shaikh during her pregnancy.

Akbar's initial response to these happy events was to make a pilgrimage on foot to Ajmer, the Chishti headquarters. But in 1571 he decided to go further, and as a mark of his respect for Shaikh Salim began to embellish the hill at Sikri with a vast mosque, and an imperial palace. As Akbar's friend and court historian, Abul Fazl, explained:

> Inasmuch as his exalted sons had taken their birth in Sikri and the God-knowing spirit of Shaikh Salim had taken possession thereof, his holy heart desired to give outward splendour to this spot which possessed spiritual grandeur. ... An order was issued that the superintendents of affairs should erect lofty buildings for the special use of the Shahinshah.

As Abul Fazl also related, the nobles of the court immediately began to construct their own houses in the vicinity and a surrounding fortification wall was erected, so that in a short time a new city arose. Following Akbar's conquest of the region of Gujarat in 1572–3, he dignified the name of his new city with the prefix 'Fatehpur', or 'City of Victory'.

The palace and the mosque stand on the top of a ridge

(*Opposite*) Khan Jahan presenting prisoners to Akbar at Fatehpur Sikri.

Fatehpur Sikri
1. palace;
2. mosque; 3. lake
area; 4. city area.

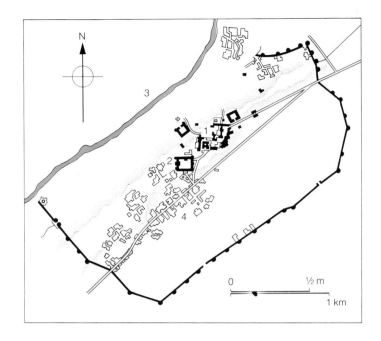

which runs in a straight line, on a diagonal to the polar axes, from south-west to north-east. Most of the city — now dwindled — lay on the south-east side of the ridge. The city and the palace together covered an area of about 5 sq km (2 sq miles). This was enclosed on three sides by the city wall, which was pierced by nine major gates; parts of the wall survive, including the gate at the north-east corner, the Agra Gate, which is still used by visitors. On the north-western side there was no wall but a large lake, now dry.

In the heyday of Fatehpur Sikri, the whole length of the road between it and Agra was flanked by a continuous market. The English merchant Ralph Fitch, who saw it at that time, said that travelling through the countryside between the two cities, one felt 'as though a man were still in a towne'. The heyday did not, however, last very long. By the time that the slightly later merchant William Finch visited Fatehpur Sikri in 1610, the city was ruined and deserted. In an unconscious reversal of Fitch's remark, he pointed to the crops sprouting over what had once been streets and commented that a man standing within the walls 'would little thinke he were in the middest of a citie'. When building operations had begun on the site in 1571, the work had progressed rapidly and lavishly, and the new city became the capital of the empire; but in 1585, after only fourteen years, Akbar and his court suddenly moved away from the new creation, and they never returned to it.

Why this should be so is one of a number of puzzles connected with Fatehpur Sikri. A traditional explanation (still sometimes accepted) is that the water supply failed. This theory is based on a remark by Finch that the supply of good water was limited and that the major sources were polluted. Although Jahangir, in his memoirs, makes a similar complaint, the theory is unconvincing as the sole — or even principal — explanation. It is hard to believe that Akbar's engineers and planners were so incompetent as to build a city without having tested the water sources; and both Jahangir and Finch, in spite of their remarks, testify to the large size and good quality of the lake to the north-west of the city, making it clear that long after the abandonment of the site, the lake still measured 22 km (14 miles) in circumference.

A more recent and alternative theory is that Akbar was called away from Fatehpur Sikri by a threat to the empire's north-west frontier, and that for this expedition Fatehpur Sikri would have been an inconveniently placed headquarters. It is true that when Akbar marched north in the autumn of 1585, he transferred his capital to Lahore; and this city remained his base for the next thirteen years as he continued to be preoccupied with campaigns in the north. The military crisis satisfactorily accounts for the initial move; it does not, of course, explain why, when the court eventually returned to the centre in 1598, it moved back to Agra rather than to Fatehpur Sikri.

In a sense, the puzzle is an artificial one. The long-term abandonment of Fatehpur Sikri was probably not the result of a deliberate decision, not a reasoned policy, and so requires no specific explanation. Abul Fazl wrote that after the initial campaign in the Punjab in 1586, many expected Akbar to return to Fatehpur Sikri rather than, as he in fact did, remain in Lahore; though not fulfilled, the very expectation shows that a return to Fatehpur Sikri was still then an option (and incidentally further refutes the theory about the water supply). Finch's picture of the desolation of Fatehpur Sikri in 1610 refers only to parts of the city, which had inevitably fallen into decay through neglect. When Jahangir visited the site in 1619 — long after its supposed abandonment — one part of the city was still inhabited, and the palace still served as the residence of a number of people including his own mother.

The abandonment was therefore neither abrupt nor total, and was not a policy adopted by necessity. The city was simply not used again as a centre for the court, and outlasted its usefulness as such. If this suggests wastefulness, it should be remembered that the Mughal builders were not noted for economy. The Mughals repeatedly poured energy and resources into architectural projects and then abandoned or even destroyed them to concentrate on new ones. The building and abandonment of Fatehpur Sikri followed this pattern; it should be seen not as a bizarre sequence requiring explanation, but as a typical exercise in Mughal prodigality.

This matter is the least of Fatehpur Sikri's riddles. The imperial complex of palace and mosque is one of the most remarkable architectural conceptions in India. But in spite of its fair state of preservation, and the wealth of contemporary writing relating to it, there are few clues to the interpretation of some of its most intriguing aspects, and it excites a continuous controversy.

THE PALACE

The palace of Fatehpur Sikri consists of a sequence of connected rectangular courtyards; these are aligned with the polar axes and so have to be grouped in a staggered formation across the top of the narrow diagonal ridge. Like most other Indian palaces of the period, it divides into three principal parts: the *zenana* or harem, the *mardana* or men's quarters, and a public area.

Approaching the complex from the east, one enters first this public area, the court of the **Diwan-i-Am**. Normally, the place of public audience is a columned hall facing a courtyard. Here, the courtyard is very large but in place of the hall is a modest pavilion, to accommodate only the emperor and his immediate attendants. The central bay of the pavilion, where the emperor sat, is penned in by large *jalis* (screens) of geometric designs.

(*Opposite below*) The Diwan-i-Am pavilion.

A door in the back of this pavilion gives access to the even larger court of the *mardana*, a spacious terrace with a

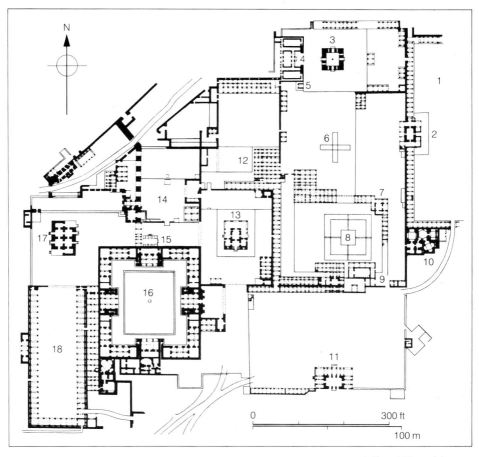

N

0   300 ft

100 m

(*Above*) Plan of the palace at Fatehpur Sikri 1,2. court and pavilion of the Diwan-i-Am; 3. Diwan-i-Khas; 4. Ankh Michauli; 5. Astrologer's seat; 6. Pachisi board; 7. Turkish Sultana's House; 8. Anup Talao; 9. Khwabgah; 10. baths; 11. Daftar Khana; 12. Panch Mahal; 13. Sunahra Makan; 14. garden; 15. Hawa Mahal; 16. Jodh Bai's Palace; 17. Birbal's House; 18. 'stables'.

variety of buildings scattered on and around it. The pavement and the buildings are all constructed of the same red sandstone. But apart from their uniform colour, what is immediately striking about the buildings is their curious architectural style, so unlike that of most other Islamic buildings in India. A certain amount has already been said about the Akbari style of the 1570s, in relation to one of the few other examples of it, the Jahangiri Mahal in the Agra Fort; but some general points may be considered again in relation to this most impressive example. As noted above, earlier Muslim buildings in India follow a basically Islamic design scheme, but incorporate a few Hindu motifs and flourishes, usually introduced by the native craftsmen whom the Muslim patrons employed. In much of the Fatehpur Sikri palace, this process of Hinduization has been exaggerated to the point where the formula is reversed: a few Islamic motifs remain as exotic details in a style in which the majority of the component parts are Hindu. In the pavilion of the Diwan-i-Am, for example, the geometric patterns of the *jalis* are the only conspicuous Islamic feature; the Diwan-i-Am, like most other apartments in the palace, is trabeate in construction and includes components such as corbel capitals and *chajjas* derived from Hindu temple architecture.

Of course, an architectural style is more than an assembly of details, and the process of Hinduization is not entirely pervasive: it is much more apparent in the selection of component parts than in the way in which they have been treated. For while the vocabulary of architectural forms and the technology have become overwhelmingly Hindu, the large-scale planning principles follow Islamic norms. The palace consists of a number of separate pavilions arranged in formal (if not always symmetrical) geometries, on a piece of level ground. This pattern is in all respects opposed to usual Hindu palace planning; it is generally supposed to derive from Arab and Central Asian tent encampments.

The northern end of the *mardana* court is dominated by a square, free-standing pavilion, identified as the **Diwan-i-Khas**. This is the most famous and enigmatic structure of the whole complex. From the outside it appears to be a two-storey building, with a *chattri* at each corner of its roof. Internally, it contains a single high hall; in the centre a column rises to half the height, and rich corbels on the column support a small round platform, which is connected to the

The Diwan-i-Khas.

corners of the building by catwalks. It is hard to see how this singular arrangement could have operated as a *diwan-i-khas* in any conventional manner: seated in the centre, the emperor would have been able to face only one part of his audience at once, and they would have to be either crowded in the small upper galleries or standing on the floor below, from where the top of the seat is not visible. The specialized design suggests that the hall performed some specific function, but what it was we cannot now be sure. It may have been of a purely symbolic nature: the single column in a square hall recalls the pattern of Hindu *mandalas*, and if this is the intended reference then the column stands for the axis of the world of the Hindu system of cosmology, and anyone who sits on top of it adapts the Hindu tradition to identify himself as the hub or focus of supreme power. The role of the pavilion may therefore have been ceremonial and ritualistic rather than practical.

The column inside the Diwan-i-Khas.

Certainly, a symbolic activity of this kind would have been consistent with some of the dominant preoccupations of Akbar in the period. For it was during the years at Fatehpur Sikri that Akbar particularly pursued his investigations in comparative religion; and these exercises led in time to the formation of his own religion, the Din Ilahi, which vested supreme spiritual authority in his own person.

The interest which Akbar took in religious and mythological enquiry helped to establish Fatehpur Sikri as a significant intellectual centre. One of the means through which the illiterate emperor pursued his studies was an institution known as the Ibadat Khana. Established in 1575, this provided a forum for debate on religious, scientific, philosophical and legal matters. The participants initially were representatives of different groups within Islam; according to the unofficial court chronicler Badauni, the discussions took place in a building containing four halls — one each for the Amirs, the Sayyids, the *ulama* and the shaikhs — and 'His Majesty would go from time to time to these various parties, and converse with them, and ascertain their thoughts'. The building itself is now lost (the tradition which identified it with the Diwan-i-Khas supposed implausibly that Badauni's talk of four halls was a metaphor for one hall's four sides).

As the discussions in the Ibadat Khana progressed, Akbar grew impatient with the quarrelsome and pedantic manners of the participants, and he reacted by broadening the discussions to include members of other faiths. Parsis (Zoroastrians), Hindus, Jains, Jews and Catholics (Jesuits from Goa) were all invited to take part. As a result the debates began to furnish Akbar with material which encouraged him to challenge and re-examine the basis of Muslim law and of religious belief itself. Such activity appalled the orthodox members of the court. The scholarly mullah Badauni, in his secret journal, complained bitterly and indignantly about the emperor's wavering commitment to Islam. He saw Akbar as a poorly educated innocent, misled by the sycophantic enthusiasm of certain courtiers; his chief villain was the official historian Abul Fazl, whom he called 'the man that set the world in flames'. This assessment was unfair both to Akbar's intellect and to Abul Fazl's integrity; both men were motivated by a distrust of authority, which rarely appeals to the clergy.

Akbar's interest in a more frivolous aspect of another culture is revealed by the pattern in the paving to the south of the Diwan-i-Khas. The great court of the *mardana* is articulated by a number of slight changes in level; in the centre is a large open space on which are inlaid the lines of the board for the game *pachisi*. This is an Indian game of great antiquity; here the board is much enlarged and Akbar perhaps used people in place of the usual small counters.

Further to the south again, and occupying the whole

The Anup Talao, with the Panch Mahal beyond.

southern half of the *mardana* court, is the private palace of the emperor. A number of pavilions are here grouped around an ornamental pool, the **Anup Talao**. Reflecting somewhat the conception of the Diwan-i-Khas, the Anup Talao has a central island linked by four bridges to its sides. On the southern side, closing the court, is a deep cloister; this conceals some inner apartments which served as the *khwabgah*, or bedroom.

To the north and east of the pool, covered walks link other pavilions, including (at the north-east corner) the exquisitely ornamented **Turkish Sultana's House**. The sloping roof of the veranda around this pavilion is carved in imitation of tiles, while the columns and external walls are carved with floral and geometric designs. Inside, a pattern of interlocking niches covers much of the walls, and the dados below have superbly naturalistic depictions of plants and animals. The latter have suffered some mutilation as the heads of the animals have been very deliberately chipped off; this must be the handiwork of an orthodox Muslim, objecting to the contravention of the law which forbids the depiction of higher forms of life. Orthodoxy on this point was rare in the court circles of Mughal India, and this mutilation was probably performed illicitly when the palace was no longer inhabited.

In addition to this vandalism, there are signs in this pavilion and in other parts of the private palace, of later changes having been made to the buildings. The covered walk leading to the Turkish Sultana's House does not join its veranda so much as collide with it, suggesting that the walk was added later and not planned for. Part of the tall cloister in front of the *khwabgah* has been fitted with an extra floor, converting its high space into two low storeys, and making the massive bracket capitals at the top of the piers seem absurd in proportion to the space which they now fill. Although the palace was occupied for only fourteen years, it is not entirely a perfect unity of conception: evidently this short period was long enough to allow for developments and changes to the original design.

The curious name of the Turkish Sultana's House relates to a traditional belief about its function which is quite mistaken: from its location we may be sure that it is a *mardana* pavilion and not the house of a queen. The identification of the functions of individual parts of the palace, and the naming of them, are matters still beset by certain confusions. Many of the existing names of the pavilions were invented by local guides in the last century, in their anxiety to please European visitors even more ignorant than themselves. Their efforts were often based on a misunderstanding about how Indian palaces were used. The Indian climate encourages an open design of room, and a space which is less firmly defined is also more adaptable in function. The absence of specialist furniture, too, meant that many pavilions of an Indian palace could be put to a variety of uses, not limited to just one. Clearly this is not true of all of its buildings: some of the

Akbar inspecting building work at Fatehpur Sikri; from a manuscript of the *Akbarnama*.

ceremonial parts of a palace, such as a *diwan-i-am*, had a single fixed function; and there are other parts, such as the baths, where the demands of one function so dictated the architectural form as to preclude all other uses. (The function of the Diwan-i-Khas here, though now mysterious, was evidently specific.) But in the residential areas of Indian palaces, the various apartments were each intended to be adaptable to a variety of purposes.

The names attached by legend to some of the pavilions of the Fatehpur Sikri palace are now generally disbelieved (they survive only as a system of reference). But those writers who propose alternative functions and names for some of the buildings ignore their adaptable character and so do not assist our understanding. For example, few now believe that the **Ankh Michauli** — the fine hall to the west of the Diwan-i-Khas — was actually used for playing Blind Man's Buff, as that given name implies; but some of those who dismiss the traditional theory suggest instead that it was used as a treasury. A treasury has a specialist role for which this hall is not well suited because of its numerous entrances; but it is perfectly adaptable as a palace pavilion in which a range of social and domestic activities might be performed.

To the west of the great court of the *mardana* lies a series of relatively smaller courts which together add up to the extensive area of the *zenana*. Not all of the parts of the *zenana* are commonly recognized as such, but an examination of the plan of the palace and of the western side of the *mardana* court reveals that a simple line divides the two main residential areas of the palace in a definite manner. The cloister to the west of the Anup Talao establishes a boundary line which is continued northwards by a blank wall up to the Ankh Michauli; the cloister and the wall limit and protect the women's quarters.

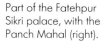

Part of the Fatehpur Sikri palace, with the Panch Mahal (right).

Standing up against the western side of this line is the distinctive pavilion known as the **Panch Mahal**. Each of its five storeys is a columned hall, and each of the flat roofs

serves as a terrace for the hall above. The storeys become progressively smaller, giving the building a pyramidal outline; the apex is a single square kiosk surmounted by a dome. The construction throughout is trabeate, creating a simple compilation of horizontals and verticals. The columns are of the Hindu temple type, with a partly octagonal and partly circular shaft, a square base and a corbel capital; many of them — and especially those on the second storey — are decorated with varied and inventive carvings, some depicting fruits. The sides of the building now appear very open, but originally the spaces between the outer columns were filled by perforated screens (of which some traces remain). The screens were necessary because the Panch Mahal was intended for the use of the women, who had to remain concealed from the more public parts of the palace: their breezy tower placed against the boundary of the *mardana* gave them a concealed vantage point from which to observe proceedings in the men's courtyard below. The view from the top still rewards the tortuous climb.

To the south-west of the Panch Mahal, standing on its own podium, is an independent *zenana* pavilion called Maryam's House or the **Sunahra Makan** ('Golden House'). It takes the latter name from the vivid murals which decorate it and which included gold colouring, now largely disintegrated. The boldest of the paintings are geometric designs, used especially on the interior ceilings; some of the paintings in the veranda are figurative.

To the south of the Sunahra Makan is the entrance to the largest single court of the *zenana*, known as **Jodh Bai's Palace**. This was the residence of a number of the emperor's principal wives. The personalised name given it is, like others, based on a misconception: *zenana* life was partly communal, and this court is designed to provide both private and shared spaces for a number of women. On the exterior, the court is enclosed by high and somewhat blank walls; the balconies at the corners allowed the residents a view out but kept the interior concealed. The court therefore provided within the *zenana* area, a place of even greater privacy, and a place which could be defended. To the left of the entrance gate is a guardroom, but this represented only a part of the court's elaborate security arrangements, as Abul Fazl described:

The inside of the Harem is guarded by sober and active

An interior of Jodh
Bai's palace.

women.... Outside of the enclosure the eunuchs are placed;
and at a proper distance, there is a guard of faithful Rajputs,
beyond whom are the porters of the gates. Besides, on all four
sides, there are guards of Nobles, Ahadis, and other troops.

Having negotiated the winding entrance through the gate,
one enters a broad square court bordered by ranges of
apartments. The centre of each side is dominated by an
engaged two-storey block. The pyramid domes on the
chattris of these blocks, and the pitched roofs covered in
turquoise tiles, contrast with the squat round domes over the
corner towers. The form of the ranges and the plan of the
court in general are closely based on a Rajput palace

tradition which includes such earlier examples as the Gujari Mahal at Gwalior (*c*. 1500) and the Raj Mandir at Orchha (1554–91). In thus drawing on Hindu precedents in its planning (as well as in its details), Jodh Bai's Palace differs from the other parts of the complex, where Islamic planning ideas have been followed.

Against the northern outside wall of Jodh Bai's palace is a **Hawa Mahal** or 'wind palace', where the women could sit to enjoy a breeze. Opposite it, to the north, are the remains of a small formal garden, intended for their further relaxation. A raised and enclosed walkway passes from the Hawa Mahal, past the garden, to the Hathi Pol (originally an important entrance to the whole complex), giving the women direct and discreet access to their own apartments from outside.

To the west stands **Birbal's House**. Again the attribution is fictitious: Raja Birbal was a colourful and influential figure in Akbar's court, but he could not have occupied a building so prominent, nor one in the middle of the *zenana*; this is another pavilion intended for the use of the women. It is dated by an inscription to 1571, and was therefore one of the first parts of the palace to be completed. It is ingeniously planned: on the ground storey there are four square chambers in a square formation; two of these are surmounted by further chambers, while the other two support terraces; and the diagonal arrangement of the upper chambers and terraces ensures that one or other of the terraces is always shaded.

Decorative carving on Birbal's House.

The stone carving which decorates this house is exceptionally crisp and rich. The deep *chajja* between the two storeys is supported by elaborate brackets with pendant bosses; below each bracket is a square-sectioned pilaster, its base decorated with a rosette contained in an ogee moulding. All of these motifs are taken directly from the Hindu temple tradition. However, much of the other decoration is Islamic, notably the geometric patterns over the surfaces of the pilasters, the pointed arches carved in relief between them, and the shallow arched niches. Above, Hindu *jarokhas* similarly consort with an Islamic arcade. In the details of the building, therefore, elements from India's two main architectural traditions are muddled together. There has been no attempt here to fuse or synthesize those sources (in spite of the popular view to the contrary): the assembly of the diverse parts has not involved any of them being changed into something new; they are simply juxtaposed in an elaborate medley.

This approach is the one which was adopted throughout most of the Fatehpur Sikri palace. The result, though arresting, is somewhat curious. The style of these buildings is like the collection of a catholic connoisseur: the various motifs and decorations are each individually excellent but they do not cohere into a unity. There has been no attempt at stylistic integrity. As a result, the style is more intriguing than satisfying. For in their original forms, the two traditions which have been used — like other architectural traditions of the world — are not just catalogues of details, to be picked from as desired. Each style has its own logic, a set of standard practices which amount to a grammar, governing the architectural vocabulary. Taking forms out of their context and mixing them with others from a different source, deprives them of the significance which comes from traditional usage. In its details, the style of Fatehpur Sikri entirely ignores the niceties of architectural grammar; it neither follows traditions, nor develops them, but plunders them. It is a cabinet of curiosities. In its defence one might say that to lack integrity is not to lack interest; and the various elements do achieve a certain limited unity through the consistent perfection of the craftsmanship and the uniform colour of the material.

We are told by Abul Fazl that Akbar took a deep interest in the building of Fatehpur Sikri; and although he was not a designer, it is reasonable to suppose that the emperor had some influence on the formation of the style. With its dominant Hindu contribution, the style could be seen as a reflection of Akbar's broader interest in Hindu thought and culture — an interest revealed by his commissioning of scholars and artists to translate and illustrate Hindu scriptures. The style has also been seen as a reflection of Akbar's policies of tolerance towards his Hindu subjects; but while clearly it reveals a measure of liberalism towards the Hindu craftsmen whom he employed, there is no evidence that Akbar was seeking to make an overtly political statement by it. Hindu architectural forms were likely to appeal to Akbar as much for their intrinsic qualities as for their cultural associations; and so by promoting their use through patronage, Akbar could have been aiming not to make a political gesture but simply to enhance his own enjoyment. Similarly, the mixture of Hindu and Islamic details was contrived not for the sake of political symbolism, perhaps, but in the hope that the combination of various excellent parts would create something of surpassing quality. The mixture suggests a parallel with the method of the emperor's religious studies, which led to the formation of his hybrid faith, the Din Ilahi.

To the south of Birbal's House, and adjacent with the western wall of Jodh Bai's Palace, is the last court of the palace, which is not the least puzzling. A rectangular open courtyard almost 90 m (300 ft) long is surrounded by small cells. With its specialized design, this court is evidently one of the parts of the palace which was intended for a specific function, but its identity eludes us. The traditional theory that the cells were stables is implausible in view of their proximity to the *zenana* buildings. They may have been intended (as more recently suggested) to accommodate the female servants of the *zenana*, or to house the palace's market.

The difficulty and the disagreement over the interpretation of this and many other parts of the palace, are a measure of the peculiarity of the palace's design. Though elements within the palace can be related to various traditions, it does not as a whole adhere to any single set of formulae and so does not present an easily readable pattern. It does not follow logically from the earlier development of Mughal architecture, and it made little impression on subsequent developments. It is in many respects a unique and still mysterious masterpiece.

THE JAMI MASJID

Separated from the palace complex by a short distance, but adjacent to it on the ridge, is the **Jami Masjid**, the new city's congregational mosque. According to an inscription, the mosque was completed in 1571, the year in which the building of the palace began, and so the mosque was evidently given priority. This is indicative of the significance attached to it; it was intended not just as a place for the population to worship in, but as an expression of the spiritual grandeur which the location was deemed to possess.

It was built on a far larger scale than any previous mosque in India: the rectangular courtyard measures 109 × 133 m (360 × 439 ft). Around the edges of the court are lines of cells for the accommodation of the mullahs. The prayer hall, on the western side, is proportionately large, though it is not one of the most harmonious of designs. Its façade has an arcade of pointed arches, interrupted and dwarfed by a towering central *iwan*, like a gate; this almost totally obscures the central dome, and the side domes lurk behind a fringe of *chattris*. The arches of the façade constitute, appropriately enough, the most emphatically Islamic statement in Fatehpur

The Jami Masjid of Fatehpur Sikri
1. prayer hall;
2. entrance from palace; 3. Shaikh Salim's tomb; 4. Islam Khan's tomb;
5. Buland Darwaza.

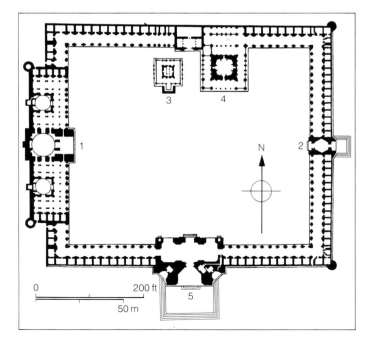

The screen of the Jami Masjid.

Sikri, but inside the hall there is a greater dependence on Hindu ideas: the domes of the side chapels are supported on Hindu corbels rather than squinches, and the ceiling is carried on columns which are of the Hindu type, though greatly elongated. In India's earliest major mosque — that of the Qutb complex in Delhi — the builders took columns from the Hindu temples which they had destroyed and piled them one above the other to achieve the desired height; here, the more sophisticated masons have adapted the traditional design to suit the new requirement.

This approach had been employed before, in the mosques of Gujarat, such as the Jami Masjid of Ahmedabad (1424). Gujarat in the 15th and 16th centuries was a sultanate independent of the Mughal empire; it is notable architecturally because its sultans went even further than the Mughals generally did in allowing the local craftsmen to introduce Hindu ideas into their mosques and tombs. In 1572–3, soon after work on Fatehpur Sikri began, Akbar conquered this region, and it is supposed that Gujarat supplied many of the craftsmen who built the new capital. There is some stylistic evidence in support of this view, and the design of the mosque interior suggests that the migration of the craftsmen began even before the military conquest.

Detail of the prayer hall of the Jami Masjid.

The lack of coherence in the façade of the prayer hall weakens it in spite of its size, and the eye is easily distracted by some buildings which stand within the courtyard, on its northern side. One of these is the marble-clad **Tomb of Shaikh Salim**. The shaikh was born in Delhi in 1479 and came to Sikri as a boy. In the middle years of his life he travelled extensively in the Muslim world, but he returned in

Shaikh Salim Chishti's tomb.

old age to live as an ascetic on the ridge by his home town. He was almost ninety when Akbar heard of him in 1568. He died soon after building operations on the new city began, and the main structure of his graceful tomb was built between 1571 and 1580. A veranda surrounds the main tomb chamber in which stands the cenotaph, covered by a canopy decorated with mother-of-pearl. It is still an object of veneration, chiefly to barren women (both Muslim and Hindu).

The dramatic serpentine struts which appear to support the *chajja* on the exterior of the building are an unusual feature; they are imitated in this case from those on the small

Stonecutters' Mosque — an older mosque built for the shaikh on the ridge — though they have earlier precedents in the architecture of Chanderi in central India. The dome was originally of red sandstone, and received its marble cladding in 1866.

The fine perforated screens which complete the marble casing and enclose the veranda, are also a later embellishment, added by Jahangir. The use of *jalis* in a tomb was common in 15th-century Gujarat, and the idea was adopted and refined in Mughal architecture. The present example was followed by the tomb of Itimad-ud-daulah in Agra. A slightly earlier example is the tomb in Gwalior of another Muslim divine of the Akbari period, Muhammad Ghaus (a building which follows Gujarati ideas in some other aspects of its arrangement and detailing). In Rajput architecture, pierced screens were introduced chiefly to ensure the seclusion of women, but their use in Mughal buildings is more varied: in the palaces they are found as a decorative motif in the *mardana* as much as in the *zenana*, and in tombs they create a suitably subdued atmosphere in the veranda, providing shade while admitting air.

They are used in this last way again in the tomb which stands immediately next to the shaikh's, to the east. This is a

(*Above*) A column of the porch of Shaikh Salim's tomb.

(*Below*) Muhammad Ghaus's tomb, Gwalior.

larger but less dominant building, because instead of dazzling white marble, it is sheathed in red sandstone, like the mosque itself. The principal of its many occupants is **Islam Khan**, a grandson of the shaikh, who became governor of Bengal in the reign of Jahangir. Other men of the shaikh's family and possibly some disciples share the tomb, while the women of the family are buried in a section of the mosque's cloister behind it.

The imperial entrance to the mosque is located on the eastern side of its courtyard — the side closest to the palace — and opposite the prayer hall. But the simple symmetry of this arrangement was disrupted by the later addition of a massive gateway in the southern side, a structure quite out of scale with the mosque to which it is attached. The **Buland Darwaza** or 'lofty gate' was added in 1575-6 in celebration of Akbar's conquest of Gujarat (the reference in an inscription to a later victory should not be taken as an indication of the date of construction). The gate rises 40 m (134 ft) above the level of the mosque court. On the outside, the builders have contrived to exaggerate its height: immediately outside one can look at it only from directly below, as there is no space to step back; in front of it, a flight of steps cascades a further 12 m (42 ft) to the road level, so that from further away it appears even larger.

In style it is somewhat dissimilar to other parts of Fatehpur Sikri. Though it has many Hindu embellishments, its severe pointed arches and the simple geometry of its basic form mark a return to the more usual approach of early Mughal architecture — to the style of Humayun's tomb, for example. This is quite calculated. The intricate surface carving of the palace's pavilions could not be translated to this sort of scale; the gate has some decorative carving but it does not rely on this for its effect: the great planes of its surfaces, the strong vertical lines of the slim towers engaged at its corners, and the deep recesses of its arches are its essential parts. All of these are visible from a great distance, and they constitute Akbar's surest assertion of power.

(*Opposite*) The Buland Darwaza.

PROVINCIAL CENTRES
MUGHAL SANCTUARIES

This account of Mughal architecture has concentrated on the three capital cities which most tourists visit, and where most of the major examples are to be found. But there survive many other examples in the provincial towns scattered throughout the former empire. Some of these have already been mentioned in passing; the following sections list a few more — buildings which should be included in any survey because, though not in a prime location, they are still among the best specimens of the Mughal style.

SRINAGAR, KASHMIR

One of the northern campaigns which occupied Akbar following his departure from Fatehpur Sikri, was the conquest of Kashmir, achieved in 1586. Much struck by the beauty of his new acquisition, the emperor visited it a number of times subsequently; and this special link was sustained by Jahangir and Shah Jahan. To the Mughals, the valley of Kashmir was an earthly paradise: the beauty of its mountain landscape and its refreshing climate offered a welcome respite from the hot plains of Hindustan. Although it was Akbar who added it to the empire's domains, and who built the **Hari Parbat Fort** overlooking Srinagar, the valley is associated most especially with Jahangir, whose love of the place amounted to an obsession. Jahangir was an ardent (and informed) lover of the natural world, and his memoirs contain a panegyric on the charms of his favourite corner of his inheritance:

> Kashmir is a garden of eternal spring, or an iron fort to a palace of kings — a delightful flower-bed, and a heart-expanding hermitage for the mendicant. Its pleasant meads and enchanting cascades are beyond all description. There are running streams and fountains beyond count ... The red rose, the violet and the narcissus grow of themselves; in the fields, there are all kinds of flowers and all sorts of sweet-scented herbs, more than can be counted. In the soul-enchanting spring, the hills and plains are filled with blossoms; the gates, the walls, the courts, the roofs, are lighted up by the torches of banquet-adorning tulips.

(*Opposite*) Jahangir boating in Kashmir.

127

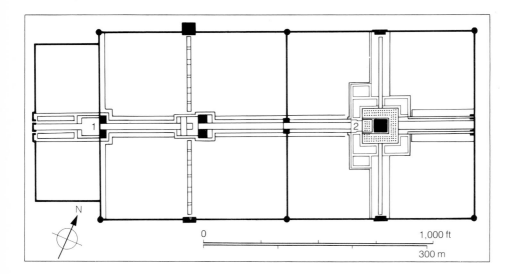

The Shalimar Bagh,
Kashmir
1. Diwan-i-Am;
2. Black Pavilion.

It was during Jahangir's reign that Srinagar was most assiduously developed as a retreat for the imperial court. Akbar had built a garden, the **Nasim Bagh** on the west bank of Dal Lake, of which little now remains. Jahangir undertook many projects and laid the foundations of the most famous of the gardens, the **Shalimar Bagh**, to the north-east of the lake.

This is the most splendid of the surviving Mughal gardens. The Persian *charbagh* tradition on which the plan of all such gardens is based, can be traced back at least to the eighth century; and it is in turn based on a Koranic idea: the Koran repeatedly asserts that heaven — the reward of the faithful — is a garden, and among the garden's specific details it mentions watercourses and fountains. By the time the Shalimar Bagh was laid out in 1619, these essential ideas had been greatly developed. The rectangular garden, some 548 m (600 yd) long, divides into three parts; these correspond to the three main areas of a Mughal palace so that the garden could function as such: there is a public garden, a private garden for the emperor, and a *zenana* garden. The three parts are arranged as an ascending sequence of terraces. The changes in height not only facilitate the flow of water, but also ensure that to someone entering the garden from below, each of the higher levels is concealed from view until it is reached. The *zenana* occupies the highest terrace,

128

which affords the women both the greatest privacy and the best view.

The public garden is at the lowest level. It was originally linked to the lake by a canal (this is now severed and the garden itself is infringed by a modern road). On the boundary between the public part and the emperor's private garden — as in the equivalent position in a palace — stands the Diwan-i-Am. Within the pavilion, a black marble throne forms an island in the water channel; this arrangement is presumably an allusion to the remark in the Koran that the streams of Paradise flow under pavilions. On this symbolic seat, the emperor presented himself to the populace.

A column base in the Black Pavilion.

The emperor's garden, at the middle level, originally contained a *diwan-i-khas*. The Black Pavilion, in the centre of the *zenana* garden was added in 1630 by Shah Jahan. This is something of an architectural caprice; its pyramidal, three-tiered roof is based on those of traditional Kashmiri wooden mosques (some examples of which may be seen in the old city of Srinagar).

It is believed that in Jahangir's time several hundred gardens fringed the borders of Dal Lake. Today, the only

The Black Pavilion in the Shalimar Bagh.

other substantial one to survive apart from the Shalimar Bagh, is the **Nishat Bagh**, located about 3 km (2 miles) to the south. Though of the same size as the other, this was divided into twelve narrow terraces (the lower parts have been destroyed, again by a road). The water flows down these terraces from pool to pool, gathering speed in the narrow channels and on the sculpted slopes (or *chadars*) which make it sputter and foam. The different overall plan reflects a different use: the top part was again a *zenana*, but the garden was not intended as an imperial palace; it was the resort of a nobleman. The builder was one Asaf Khan (perhaps Nur Jahan's brother, or a Kashmiri governor of the same name). The pavilions have not survived well, though the octagonal ones near the north and east corners were fine.

The view from the Nishat Bagh towards the lake.

The Nishat Bagh is notable mainly for the breath-taking beauty and the ingenious use of its natural setting. The view up the terraces is completed by the vast backdrop of the

mountains, while the view down from the top leads the eye to the open expanse of the surface of the lake. This attempt to relate to the landscape is a point of distinction between the Kashmir gardens and those in the palaces on the plains, which otherwise share the same essential principles of design. The Islamic garden traditionally is an oasis; it is inward-looking and protected from the hostile environment by a wall. Here, the formal garden is merely an episode in the larger natural one.

Another point of distinction is the method of planting. In the formal gardens of the palaces, such as the Anguri Bagh in the Agra fort, the planting was low, using only flowers, so as not to obscure the architectural lines. In the tomb gardens, and even more in the Kashmir gardens, with the increase in scale, larger shrubs and trees were used as well. Among the trees used here were the *chenar* or Oriental plane (perhaps introduced into Kashmir by the Mughals), the aspen, the cypress, and fruit trees including apple, quince and plum. Flowers were still important too. The Mughals' favourite flowers in spring were irises, narcissi, crown imperials and tulips; these gave way in summer to jasmine, delphiniums, peonies and roses.

Other vestiges of Mughal rule in Srinagar include the **Pathar Masjid**, a small stone mosque built in the old city by Nur Jahan.

LAHORE
(PAKISTAN)

The city of Lahore was at various times used as the main residence of the court during the Mughal period, and so ranks in importance not far behind the other cities described. It contains a large number and wide variety of Mughal buildings — or the remains of them, for some have not fared well. Though Lahore is no longer within the borders of India, and is less visited by tourists than the other Mughal cities, the more remarkable buildings within it must receive mention.

Some of the buildings in and around the city — and especially some of those built during the reign of Shah Jahan — show a higher degree of Persian influence than do Mughal buildings elsewhere. This reflects the proximity of the Punjab to the rival empire (and incidentally reflects how much designs depended on local craftsmen rather than an emperor's taste). The main aspect of the influence is the use of highly coloured glazed tile decoration, known as *kashi*. It

Lahore Fort
1. Masti Darwaza;
2. Bari Khwabgah;
3. Diwan-i-Am;
4. Choti Khwabgah;
5. Khilat Khana;
6. Moti Masjid;
7. Mussaman Burj;
8. Sheesh Mahal;
9. Naulakha;
10. Hathi Pol.

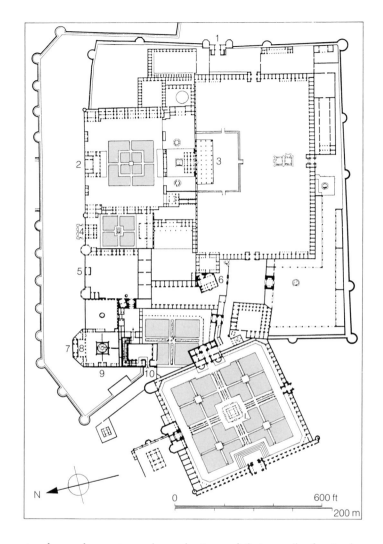

is a form of mosaic work: each piece of tile is small, of a single colour, and cut to a shape determined by the design; and the pieces are stuck to the wall surface with cement.

The most spectacular example of this work is to be found on the outer walls of the **Fort**. The fort of Lahore was built, and the palaces within it were begun, during the reign of Akbar. It is contemporary with the Agra fort and was designed on similar lines, though it is rather smaller, being a rough rectangle measuring 365 × 304 m (1,200 × 1,000 ft).

132

It is now usually entered through the Hathi Pol (or 'elephant gate') on the western side. It is around this gate and on the fort's northern wall that the tile decoration was added, during Shah Jahan's reign. Though the technique was imported from Persia, the subject-matter shows a marked Hindu influence (perhaps from the palace at Gwalior) for much of it is figurative: the motifs include elephant fights and other sporting scenes, as well as the usual Islamic repertoire of geometric and floral patterns.

The palace apartments within were built over a long period, Akbar's original scheme (as in the Agra fort) having been substantially altered by his successors. At a later date, the fort was used and further altered by the Sikhs. These

Palace apartments in Lahore Fort.

changes have not disrupted the essentially formal layout, a characteristic feature of Mughal palace design. The oldest surviving part of the palace lies in the north-east corner of the fort. The ranges which face each other across a square were probably built by Akbar; they are of red sandstone and have richly carved Hindu-style brackets, like Akbar's palace in Agra. On the northern side of the same court is a pavilion known as the Bari Khwabgah ('large bedroom'); this is attributed to Jahangir though it has evidently been modified. To the west lies a similar court, though smaller and better preserved, with a formal garden in its centre. On its northern side is the white marble Choti Khwabgah ('little bedroom') built by Shah Jahan.

To the south of these two courts is the expansive court of the Diwan-i-Am: as in other Mughal palaces, the main ceremonial area is set apart from and conceals the line of private apartments. The hall of the Diwan-i-Am itself belongs to various periods: the row of chambers at the back was built by Jahangir; the columned hall in front was added by Shah Jahan in 1627; and the whole was altered by the Sikhs. Near the north-west corner of the court is Jahangir's small Moti Masjid (or 'pearl mosque'). It is built of white marble, like its namesakes added to the Agra fort by Shah Jahan and the Delhi fort by Aurangzeb.

The finest of the palace apartments, with the most intricate decoration, are grouped together in the Mussaman Burj added by Shah Jahan at the north-west corner of the fort. These apartments include the half-octagonal Sheesh Mahal, decorated (as that name implies) with mirror-work, and also some *pietra dura*. Close by is the Naulakha, a small marble pavilion with a *bangaldar* roof. Both have been somewhat disfigured by later accretions, but still give an idea of Mughal decoration at the height of its sophistication.

Adjacent to the fort, on the western side, is the **Badshahi Masjid**, built by Aurangzeb in 1674 to house a number of relics including a hair of the Prophet. The design of this large mosque is based on the Jami Masjid in Delhi, but it departs from that model in having more minarets — one at each corner of the prayer hall, and one at each corner of the *sahn*, making eight in total. It is further distinguished from its model by a certain feebleness of form, typical of the later Mughal period. The mouldings on the façade of the prayer hall are shallow, and the white line markings are a superficial

ornament without vigour. Still, the simple red and white colour scheme follows a long-established tradition and lends the building a customary stately grandeur.

The Badshahi Mosque seen from the Fort.

In this respect, it differs radically from the other large mosque in Lahore — **Wazir Khan's Mosque**, situated in the eastern quarter of the old walled city. This was built in 1634 by Shah Jahan's governor of Lahore. Its interior and exterior surfaces are covered in colour. Some of the surfaces are painted; others are decorated with the glazed tile mosaic, or *kashi*-work. The riot of colour largely overpowers the architectural volumes, though the entrance gate is a strong and satisfying composition. The court is dominated by four minarets, in the pattern later adopted in Aurangzeb's mosque.

Also within the city, of Mughal date and worth visiting, is the **Tomb of Anarkali** (1615) — a woman declared by legend to have been loved by Jahangir and put to death for the privilege.

Eight kilometres (5 miles) to the east of the city is a spacious Mughal garden, the **Shalimar Bagh**. This was laid out by the administrator Ali Mardan Khan on the orders of Shah Jahan, in 1637. The rectangular enclosure is over 457 m (500 yd)

135

The Shalimar Bagh, Lahore.

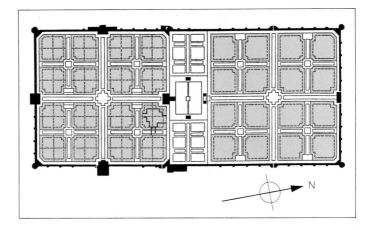

long and contains two *charbaghs* joined by a narrow terrace. Each of these three parts is on a different level, so that — as in the garden's namesake in Kashmir — the upper parts are concealed from the view of anyone entering from below, and the highest part could be used as an imperial *zenana*. The pavilions have lost their marble cladding, but the garden is still a pleasant resort.

A similar distance outside the city to the north, at Shahdara, is the **Tomb of Jahangir**. This stands in a garden which had existed previously, and which belonged to the empress Nur Jahan, by whom the tomb was commissioned in 1627. The design is based on the tomb of the empress's father, Itimad-ud-daulah, in Agra, but the composition is even less successful, exaggerating the weaknesses of the model. The central pavilion is yet smaller in relation to the substructure on which it stands, and is dwarfed by the minarets at the corners. It quite fails to provide an adequate main focus; indeed the effect of this tiny pavilion on its huge podium is more than slightly absurd. Some of the detailing, however — especially the carving and *pietra dura* — is of the usual superb quality. Close by is the **Tomb of Asaf Khan** (Nur Jahan's brother) who died in 1641. Octagonal in form, it has lost most of the *kashi* tiles which once adorned it.

Forty-one kilometres (26 miles) to the west of Lahore, at **Sheikhupura**, is a small Mughal resort consisting of a fort and a hunting lodge. This complex was built by Jahangir, and later used and embellished by Dara Shukoh (the eldest son of Shah Jahan). Beyond the complex is a tank in which a causeway leads to the Hiran Minar, an elegant octagonal tower built by Jahangir in memory of a pet deer.

Standing at the confluence of the Ganges and the Jumna, Allahabad is a city of ancient origin, but it was refounded by Akbar. As already mentioned, Akbar built the fort and the palace within it in 1583; these have been badly damaged (and are not now open to the public).

Of greater interest, therefore, is the garden known as the **Khusrau Bagh** close to the railway station. It is entered through an imposing gateway. The garden was originally built for Prince Salim (the future Jahangir) but he gave it to his eldest son, Khusrau, after whom it is now named. In his youth, in the last years of Akbar's reign, Khusrau was favoured by a party at court for the succession, in preference to his unstable and often drunk father. In the event, Jahangir succeeded, but two years later Khusrau rebelled against his father. He was quickly captured, and he was imprisoned in his garden in Allahabad. When he repeated the exercise as

ALLAHABAD
AND SASARAM

Part of the Palace in the Fort of Allahabad; aquatint by Thomas Daniell, 1795.

soon as he was released, Jahangir had him blinded and kept in chains. In this pitiful state, Khusrau continued for many years, but he later partially recovered his sight; and he was again favoured by some at court for the succession, against the claims of his energetic younger brother, Shah Jahan, especially when Shah Jahan was himself in revolt in the early 1620s. Khusrau died, however, while in the care of his rival brother in 1621. His body was brought back to his garden for burial.

His tomb is the most easterly of the group of three in the garden. The tomb to its west is believed to be that of his sister; and the third, of trabeate construction, is the tomb of his mother — a Rajput princess from Amber.

Two hundred and forty kilometres (150 miles) further east from Allahabad, in the state of Bihar, is Sasaram. This was the capital of the eastern sultanate established by the Afghan adventurer Sher Shah Sur — the man who ejected Humayun from the Delhi throne in 1540, inaugurated a regime which temporarily replaced the Mughals, and completed Delhi's Purana Qila (for an account of his career, see pp. 40–1). Sasaram has now dwindled to a small and particularly unattractive town, but it contains a building which, in terms of compositional harmony and power of form, is one of the finest works of architecture in India: **Sher Shah's Tomb**. Built of buff sandstone, it stands on an island in the middle of a huge artificial tank, and is approached by a causeway from the northern bank.

The form of the tomb itself is based on a type which had long been in use in Delhi. The principal features of this type include the octagonal plan, the deep veranda with three tall pointed arches on each side, and the large but low central dome which is usually surrounded by *chattris*. This pattern is often associated with Delhi's Lodi sultans; in fact its origins lie in an earlier period and it had been developed to its mature form by the Sayyid sultans early in the 15th century. Most of the tombs of the ensuing Lodi period are square in plan, the one notable exception, which revived the Sayyid type, being the tomb of Sikander Lodi (1517). This was the first in a sequence of revivals: the others include — apart from Sher Shah's tomb — the tomb of Isa Khan, a nobleman at the Sur court (1547) and the tomb of Adham Khan (1562), both in Delhi.

The location of Sher Shah's tomb in his former capital at

Sasaram suggests that it was built before the sultan took possession of Delhi in 1540. The adoption of a central, imperial style may be taken as a sign of his pretensions, though because that style was a somewhat outmoded one it reflects also his provincial context. After he had taken Delhi, and its craftsmen became his subjects, his building projects became more progressive.

But though the basis of its design was a well-tried formula, the tomb in Sasaram lifted the tradition onto a higher plane, and it far exceeds its antecedents in grandeur. To begin with, it is vast, being 45 m (150 ft) high and 76 m (250 ft) across. And compared with its models, it contains two extra storeys: above the veranda rises a wall, the surfaces of which are punctuated by the *chattris* in front: and above is another, lower wall and another row of *chattris*, below the dome. The podium with its surrounding wall, gives the tomb a grand setting, recalling the fortified tombs of the early Delhi sultans. (The tomb stands at a slightly awkward angle on the podium — the result of the need to correct an error of alignment in the construction of the podium, and ensure that one side of the tomb faces Mecca.) The steps down into the water are also an important part of the composition, providing a

Sher Shah Sur's tomb, Sasaram.

gentle transition between the vertical walls and the surface of the water. Most important of all, though, is the placing of this ensemble in the centre of a tank. This setting gives it a magical quality, as the great pile of masonry appears to float, or to balance on its own reflection. The calm water isolates the building from its surroundings, and enhances the dignity and repose which are so suitable to its purpose.

Closer to the centre of the town, is the **Tomb of Hasan Khan Sur**, Sher Shah's father. Built a little earlier (*c.* 1535), this is based on the same models and shows a stage of experimentation with the form which led to the later work. It stands in a garden rather than in a tank, and has only one extra storey — a somewhat grim one, because not relieved by *chattris*. Still, its simpler form lends it a certain sober dignity.

AJMER

Though situated in the heart of Rajasthan where it was surrounded by Rajput kingdoms, Ajmer has Islamic associations as old as Delhi's: having previously been one of the major Rajput capitals, it was conquered by Muhammad of

Ajmer Fort

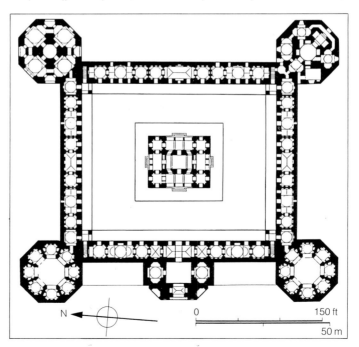

N ←

0   150 ft

50 m

The pavilions at Anar Sagar, Ajmer.

Ghur at the end of the 12th century. Among its older monuments is the Arhai-din-ka-jhonpra, a mosque built at the same time as the Qutb mosque in Delhi (*c*. 1200) and similarly incorporating fragments of destroyed temples, including in this case some exquisite carved ceilings from Jain temples. Some of the arches in the front of the prayer hall are of a cusped form — one of the prototypes of the mature form which is so ubiquitous in the architecture of Shah Jahan. The city contains also the *dargah* or burial place of the saint Kwhaja Muin-ud-din (d. 1256) of the Chishti order, and was frequently visited by Akbar on that account. It was further important in the Mughal period as the capital of a province of the empire.

In 1570, Akbar ordered the construction of a small **Fort** and palace within the city. The fort is rectangular, with a gate in the middle of its western side and an octagonal bastion at each corner; inside is a courtyard with a rectangular pavilion in the centre. The plan has all the tidiness and simplicity of a model, but the details of the buildings are highly sophisticated. The pavilion is built of a yellow stone. The division of its internal space in a pattern of nine sections is based on a Hindu *mandala*; and, as in other Mughal buildings of the 1570s, many of the details (such as the brackets supporting the *chajja*) are taken directly from Hindu sources. The merlons on the parapet and the blind arches incised on the façades are Islamic forms. The carved decoration is typically crisp, and much of it is elegant and restrained — especially the single grooves running down the edges of the plain square piers. The gate of the fort is also an interesting if not fully resolved composition: the design is somewhat fragmented by the use of different coloured stones; but it has some fine details, including the *jalis* filling the arch above the trabeate entrance.

To the north of the city is an artificial lake called **Anar Sagar**. The dam itself is of ancient origin, but the string of pavilions along the top of it was added by Shah Jahan. There are four pavilions, of assorted sizes, each sheathed in white marble. The absence of cusped arches and the use of lintels with elaborate brackets, suggest that they were built early in Shah Jahan's reign — that they represent a point of transition between early Mughal design and the mature style of Shah Jahan's main palaces. The pavilions provided a place for relaxation, where the emperor and his entourage could sit and admire the lake, enjoying a breeze. They are most beautiful as the sun sets and catches the marble, turning each pavilion into a brilliant yellow flame.

GLOSSARY

bagh   garden
bangaldar   'Bengali'; roof with curved surfaces and eaves
bund   dam
burj   tower, bastion
chadar   sloping chute for water
chajja   sloping dripstone in place of eaves
charbagh   'fourfold garden'; formal garden quartered by water channels
chattri   domed kiosk (also a Rajput cenotaph, which commonly takes this form)
chowk   courtyard or other open space
chunam   polished lime plaster
dargah   burial place of a Muslim saint
diwan-i-am   hall of public audience
diwan-i-khas   hall of private audience
hammam   baths
hauz   tank for ablutions in the courtyard of a mosque
iwan   large arched recess, especially one containing an entrance
jali   perforated stone screen
jami   Friday; Jami Masjid: principal mosque of a city, used by a large congregation for Friday prayer
jarokha   small balcony with columns supporting a hood
khana   dwelling, room, apartment
khwabgah   bedroom
liwan   prayer hall or covered part of a mosque
madrasa   Muslim school
mahal   palace, or apartment within a palace
mandala   Hindu cosmological diagram
mardana   men's quarters in a palace
masjid   'place of prostration'; mosque
mihrab   arched recess which denotes the qibla (*q.v.*)
minbar   pulpit (formed of steps) in a mosque
mullah   one learned in Islamic theology; priest
muqarnas   moulding with a web of miniature vaults
naqqar khana   drum house, especially over a gate

pol   gate
purdah   'curtain'; the seclusion of women
qibla   the direction of Mecca and hence of Muslim prayer
qila   fort
riwaq   cloister bordering the courtyard of a mosque
sagar   lake
sahn   courtyard of a mosque
shaikh   Muslim holy man or saint
sheesh mahal   'glass palace'; apartment decorated with mirror-work
ulama   plural of *alim*: one learned in Islamic canon law
zenana   women's quarters in a palace or house

English architectural terms

arcuate   of construction: involving the use of true arches, with radiating voussoirs (*q.v.*) *cf.* trabeate
drum   circular or octagonal base (or neck) supporting a dome
engaged   of a column: attached to a wall, not free-standing
four-centred   of an arch: composed of four arcs, with a shallow arc on each side of the central point and a tight arc at each extremity (e.g. a Tudor arch)
hypostyle   of a hall: with ceiling supported by columns, not walls
intrados   underside or inner curve of an arch
merlon   solid part between spaces of a battlement
pietra dura   inlay of (esp. semi-precious) stones in a stone background
squinch   arched vault across an interior corner, helping to carry the dome or drum (*q.v.*)
trabeate   of construction: involving post and beam elements only, with no true arches. *cf.* arcuate
voussoir   one of a series of wedge-shaped stones forming an arch

CHRONOLOGY

BABUR	r. 1526–30	
	Delhi	Madhi Masjid
		Shaikh Yusuf Qattal's Tomb (1527)
	Agra	Rambagh
HUMAYUN	r. 1530–56	
	(and the Sur sultans, r. 1540–55)	
	Delhi	Jamali Kamali Mosque and Tomb (1528–36)
		Imam Zamin's Tomb (1537)
	Sasaram	Hasan Khan's Tomb (*c.* 1535)
		Sher Shah's Tomb (*c.* 1540)
	Delhi	Purana Qila (*c.* 1530–45)
		Qala-i-Kuhna Masjid (1541)
		Sher Mandal (*c.* 1541)
		Gate of Sher Shah's wall (1540s)
		Salimgarh (1546)
		Isa Khan's Mosque and Tomb (1547)
		Sabz Burj, Nila Gumbad
		Bu Halima's Garden
AKBAR	r. 1556–1605	
	Delhi	Humayun's Tomb (1560s)
		Arab Sarai (1560s)
		Khair-ul Manazil Masjid (1561)
		Adham Khan's Tomb (*c.* 1562)
		Dargah of Nizam-ud-din (1562 and after)
		Ataga Khan's Tomb (1566)
		Afsarwala Mosque and Tomb (1566)
	Agra	Agra Fort, incl. Amar Singh Gate, Jahangiri Mahal (1565–70)
	Ajmer	Ajmer Fort and Pavilion (1570–2)
	Lahore	Lahore Fort and Palace
	Fatehpur Sikri	Jami Masjid (1571)
		Shaikh Salim Chishti's Tomb (1571–80)
		Islam Khan's Tomb
		Palace (1571–85)
		Buland Darwaza (1575–6)
	Allahabad	Allahabad Fort and Palace (1583)
	Gwalior	Muhammad Ghaus's Tomb
	Srinagar	Hari Parbat Fort (1586)
		Nasim Bagh
	Delhi	Barber's Tomb (1590)
JAHANGIR	r. 1605–27	
	Agra	Akbar's Tomb, Sikandra (1605–12)

		Lahore	Anarkali's Tomb (1615)

Lahore   Anarkali's Tomb (1615)
Buildings in Lahore Fort, incl. Moti Masjid, Bari Khwabgah
Sheikhupura complex

Srinagar   Shalimar Bagh (1619)
Nishat Bagh, Pathar Masjid

Allahabad   Khusrau's Tomb (c. 1621)
Agra   Itimad-ud-daulah's Tomb (1622–8)
Delhi   Chaunsath Khamba (1623)
Khan-i-Khanan's Tomb (c. 1626)

Lahore   Jahangir's Tomb (1627)

SHAH JAHAN   r. 1627–1658

Ajmer   Anar Sagar Pavilions
Agra   Palaces in Agra Fort, incl. Anguri Bagh, Khas Mahal, Diwan-i-Khas, Diwan-i-Am (1627–38)
Taj Mahal (1631–52)

Srinagar   Black Pavilion (Shalimar Bagh, 1630)
Lahore   Wazir Khan's Mosque (1634)
Shalimar Bagh (1637)
Palaces in Lahore Fort, incl. Choti Khwabgah, Diwan-i-Am, Mussaman Burj
Asaf Khan's Tomb (c. 1641)

Delhi   Shahjahanabad (1638–48)
Red Fort and Palace (1639–48)

Agra   Chini ka Rauza (c. 1639)
Jami Masjid (1648)

Delhi   Jami Masjid (1650–6)
Fatehpuri Masjid (1650)

Agra   Moti Masjid (Agra Fort, 1654)

AURANGZEB   r. 1658–1707

Delhi   Moti Masjid (Delhi Fort, 1659)
Burj-i-Shamali (Delhi Fort)

Lahore   Badshahi Mosque (1674)
Aurangabad   Bibi ka Maqbara (1678)

Delhi   Zinat-ul-Masjid (1710)
Safdar Jang's Tomb (1753–4)
Zafar Mahal, Hira Mahal (Delhi Fort, 1842)
Gate to Zafar Mahal (Mehrauli, c. 1850)

SELECT BIBLIOGRAPHY

Bernier, François, *Travels in the Mogul Empire AD 1656-1668*, (Paris, 1670), transl. Archibald Constable, 1891, revised Oxford, 1914

Beveridge, Annette S. (transl.), *The Babur-nama in English*, 2 vols, London, 1921

Beveridge, H. (transl.), *The Akbar Nama of Abu-l-Fazl*, 3 vols, Calcutta, 1907-21

Blochmann, H., and H.S. Jarrett (transl.), *The Ain I Akbari by Abul Fazl Allami*, 3 vols, Calcutta, 1873-94

Brand, Michael, and Glenn D. Lowry, *Akbar's India: Art from the Mughal City of Victory*, New York, 1985

— (eds), *Fatehpur Sikri*, Bombay, 1987

Brown, Percy, *Indian Architecture (Islamic Period)*, Bombay, 1942

Crowe, Sylvia, Sheila Haywood etc., *The Gardens of Mughul India*, London, 1972

Elliot, H.M., and John Dowson (eds), *The History of India as Told by its own Historians*, Vol VII, London, 1877

Fergusson, James, *History of Indian and Eastern Architecture*, Vol. 2, revised London, 1910

Fonseca, Rory, 'The Walled City of Old Delhi', *Shelter and Society*, ed. Paul Oliver, London, 1969

Foster, William (ed.), *Early Travels in India 1583-1619*, Oxford, 1921

Gascoigne, Bamber, *The Great Moghuls*, London, 1971

Gray, Basil (ed.), *The Arts of India*, Oxford, 1981

Hambly, Gavin, *Cities of Mughul India*, London, 1968

Havell, E.B., *A Handbook to Agra and the Taj, Sikandra, Fatehpur Sikri and the Neighbourhood*, 2nd ed. London, 1912

Hoag, John D., *Islamic Architecture*, London, 1987

Jairazbhoy, R.A., *An Outline of Islamic Architecture*, London, 1972

Keene, H.G., *A Handbook for Visitors to Delhi*, 4th ed. Calcutta, 1882

Koch, Ebba, *Shah Jahan and Orpheus*, Graz, 1988

Lowe, W.H. (transl.), *Muntakhabut-Tawarikh by Al-Badaoni*, Vol. 2, Calcutta, 1884

Moynihan, Elizabeth, *Paradise as a Garden in Persia and Mughal India*, London, 1982

Nath, R., *The Immortal Taj Mahal: The Evolution of the Tomb in Mughal Architecture*, Bombay, 1972

— *Monuments of Delhi*, New Delhi. 1979 [A translation of Ahmad Khan Saiyid, *Atharal Sanadid*, 1846]

Qaisar, Ahsan Jan, *Building Construction in Mughal India*, Delhi, 1988

Reuther, Oscar, *Indische Palaste und Wohnhauser*, Berlin, 1925

Rizvi, Saiyid Athar Abbas, *Fatehpur Sikri*, New Delhi, 1972

— and V.J. Flynn, *Fatehpur Sikri*, Bombay, 1975

Rogers, Alexander (transl.), *The Tuzuk-i-Jahangiri or Memoirs of Jahangir*, 2 vols, London, 1909-14

Sanderson, Gordon, *A Guide to the Buildings and Gardens, Delhi Fort*, 4th ed. Delhi, 1937

Sharma, Y.D., *Delhi and its Neighbourhood*, New Delhi, 1982

Smith, Edmund W., *The Moghul Architecture of Fathpur Sikri*, 4 vols, Allahabad, 1894-8

— *Moghul Colour Decoration of Agra*, Allahabad, 1901

Spear, Percival, *A History of India*, Vol. 2, Harmondsworth, 1965

Stephen, Carr, *The Archaeology and Monumental Remains of Delhi*, Calcutta, 1876

Tillotson, G.H.R., *The Rajput Palaces: The Development of an Architectural Style, 1450-1750*, London, 1987

Victoria and Albert Museum, *The Indian Heritage: Court Life and Arts under Mughal Rule*, London, 1982

Villiers Stuart, C.M., *Gardens of the Great Mughals*, London, 1913

Volwahsen, Andreas, *Living Architecture: Islamic Indian*, London, 1970

Watson, Francis, *A Concise History of India*, London, 1979

Welch, Stuart Cary, *The Art of Mughal India*, New York, 1963

ACKNOWLEDGEMENTS

Photographs
The American Institute of Indian Studies: pp. 87, 98 (top), 139; The author: pp. 4, 21, 24, 31, 35, 38, 40 (top), 42, 47, 48, 49, 50, 66, 67, 68, 69, 74, 75, 80, 90 (bottom), 96 (left), 107, 114, 116, 117, 121 (top & right), 123 (bottom), 129 (bottom), 141; British Library (India Office Library): pp. 19, 84, 137; reproduced by courtesy of the Trustees of the British Museum: pp. 60, 126; The J. Allan Cash Photo Library: pp. 29, 57, 61, 70, 111, 122; Chester Beatty Library, Dublin: p. 14; Fitzwilliam Museum, Cambridge: p. 17; Christina Gascoigne: pp. vi, 39, 40 (left), 81, 89, 90 (top), 101, 129 (top), 133; Patricio Goycolea/The Hutchison Library: jacket photo; Tom Hanley p. 135; Robert Harding Picture Library: pp. 123 (right) (photo: Christina Gascoigne), 124; Government of India Tourist Office: pp. 58, 96 (right); A. F. Kersting: pp. ix, 26, 43, 52, 62 (top & left), 63, 65, 83, 92, 109 (top); The MacQuitty International Photographic Collection: pp. 98 (bottom), 109 (bottom), 130; Ann & Bury Peerless Slide Resources & Picture Library: pp. 36, 77; B. Norman/Sheridan Photo Library: p. 33; by courtesy of the Board of Trustees of the Victoria & Albert Museum: pp. 6, 8, 11, 25, 102, 113.

Plans
The following sources have provided the basis for certain maps and plans in this book and the author and publishers acknowledge with gratitude permission from the relevant copyright-holders for their use.
    The Archaeological Survey of India: p. 45; John Murray (Publishers) Ltd from *A Handbook for Travellers in India* by L. F. Rushbrook Williams: p. 44; Office du Livre, Fribourg from *Living Architecture: Islamic India* by Andreas Volwahsen: p. 107; D. B. Taraporevala Sons & Co. Private Ltd, Bombay from *Indian Architecture (Volume II: Islamic Period)* by Percy Brown: p. 54.

Every effort has been made to trace copyright-holders; it is hoped that any omission will be excused.

INDEX